The
Small Town and
Country Church

The
Small Town
and
Country Church

Edwin A. Hunter

NEW YORK   ABINGDON-COKESBURY PRESS   NASHVILLE

THE SMALL TOWN AND COUNTRY CHURCH

Preface

THIS BOOK is based on the Slover Lectures which were delivered at Southwestern University, Georgetown, Texas, in July, 1946. They were undertaken with the hope of dignifying and magnifying the importance of our rural work and of bringing to pastors and leaders a new sense of responsibility for service in the rural field. They also attempt to make some practical suggestions as to the scope and nature of a rural church program.

As the government classes all communities of less than 2,500 people as rural, and most denominational boards and other agencies make a similar classification, the church in the small town has always been kept in mind along with the church in the open country.

The approach is not that of a philosopher, scientist, sociologist, or technical expert of any kind. It is that of a minister keenly interested in what is called our rural problem. I do not claim to be an authority on rural work. I have simply sought to bring together out of my reading and field experience such programs and ideas as may be helpful and workable, with some adaptations, in many situations.

The United States Department of Agriculture was most helpful in the preparation of this material. Other governmental departments were likewise most gracious in their co-operation. The help rendered and the information given by these departments have given me a much larger appreciation of what the government is really trying to do for rural America.

A diligent effort has been made to give proper acknowledgment to all the authors and writers who have been quoted freely. Without their advance thinking and writing, and information gathered from the *Christian Rural Fellowship Bulletin*, the *Methodist Rural Fellowship Bulletin*, the *Town and Country Church Bulletin*, and other periodicals, the preparation of this book would have been difficult indeed.

Grateful recognition is given to the innumerable correspondents who have been eager to make whatever contributions they could to a work which has had as its sole objective the strengthening and enriching of our rural church program.

I am appreciative also of the recognition which Dr. J. N. R. Score, president of Southwestern University, has given the rural pastors and churches in inviting the presentation of the lectures.

And lastly I am more indebted to my wife, Enola Polhemus Hunter, than to any other person for her continuous encouragement and inspiration and for the many laborious hours which she spent helping in the assembling of material and in correcting and preparing the manuscript for publication. Without her interest and co-operation this task would have been impossible.

EDWIN A. HUNTER

Contents

CHAPTER I

The Church and Rural America

THE TIME has come for our churches to awake to their responsibility and opportunity in rural America. There was a time when a Sunday preaching service and a church-school service seemed to suffice, but that day has passed. We must have a new and enlarged program of service to meet the needs of this day in which we live.

Our churches should be interested in rural America because America's most rugged moral and spiritual leadership in both state and church across the years has come from the country.

Let us look at the ministry. Mark A. May has made a most informing study of American ministers, which has been published in four volumes under the title *The Education of American Ministers.* In the second volume he calls attention to the fact that 48.4 per cent of our ministers spent their formative years in communities of less than 1,000; that 14.4 per cent came from towns of 1,000 to 25,000; that 25.6 per cent came from cities of 25,000 to 100,000; and that only 12 per cent have come from cities of over 100,000 population. According to this study practically one half of our ministers have come from small town and circuit churches in communities of less than 1,000 people. Since our government classes all communities of less than 2,500 population as rural, it is evident that considerably more than one half of all our ministers come from rural areas.

Some have contended that, while this has been true in the past, it likely would not be true today. That we might know the background of present-day theological students, a questionnaire was addressed to five hundred seminary students attending schools in various parts of the United States. Their replies indicate that 54 per cent were born in communities of less than 2,500 population, 45.4 per cent in communities of less than 1,000 people. This survey is not broad enough to be absolutely conclusive, but these figures indicate very slight change, if any, in the ratio between the number entering the ministry from rural and urban areas.

Sixty-seven college presidents were polled. Sixty-three replied to our questionnaire. Fifty-three of them were born in communities of less than 2,500 population, or in strictly rural areas. Only ten were born in communities of over 2,500 people.

A poll of certain other distinguished groups was also taken. Replies from fifty-eight United States senators indicate that forty-one of them were born in communities of less than 2,500 people. This is 70 per cent of all who replied.

Replies from all the active members of the United States Supreme Court indicate that they were all born in communities of less than 2,500 people except Justice Felix Frankfurter, who was born in Vienna, Austria.

Most of the justices of the supreme courts of the states were born in communities of less than 2,500.

Thirty-five of our present governors were born in communities of less than 2,500; twenty-one of them in communities of less than 1,000 people.

In view of these amazing facts, is it not reasonable to assume that the type of leadership we have in both church and state tomorrow will depend very largely upon what we do with the rural church today? If the country areas are allowed to deteriorate, to degenerate, it must mean an inferior moral and spiritual leadership in both church and state tomorrow.

Then again, Malcolm Dana declares that 70 per cent of all those joining our city churches by transfer of membership, and 70 per cent of the official boards in most of our great city churches, come from small town and circuit churches in strictly rural areas, where they got their first religious impressions and their first training in leadership. These percentages were tested this year in a number of our leading churches, and it was found that they hold true.

The country church cannot be saved without the sympathy, understanding, prayers, co-operation, and material help of the city church. It is also true that the city church cannot be saved without the help, the contributions, and the converts of the country church. The church which captures and converts the countryside today will be the strong city church tomorrow; for rural converts, when they move to town, will join the church which has ministered to them in the country.

11

Emblazoned on the front of the Union Station in Washington, D. C., is this inscription:

THE FARM, BEST HOME OF THE FAMILY, MAIN SOURCE OF NATIONAL WEALTH, FOUNDATION OF CIVILIZED SOCIETY, THE NATURAL PROVIDENCE

Why these words were inscribed upon a railway station I do not know, but they are significant words.

"The Farm, Best Home of the Family." The church has here another reason for being interested in rural America. The church is interested in the best homes possible for its families. Rural areas and farm life offer the best opportunities for the development of ideal family life and the cultivation of those character traits which are necessary for our national life.

The Christian home is certainly one of the cornerstones of a Christian civilization. Dr. Mark A. Dawber writing in this connection says:

Everything hinges on our ability to maintain in America something of that basis of stability, economic, social, moral, spiritual, that will insure the continuity of this institution. To date in our history the farm has proved itself as the one vocation, or better still, way of life, that has provided those elements that go into the creation, conservation and continuity of the home and family. Whatever happens to destroy these values is a matter of serious concern for our national life.[1]

If these things are true, both the church and the nation have a great stake in rural life.

Realizing that cities are not reproducing themselves

[1] *Christian Rural Fellowship Bulletin*, June, 1940.

and that "children are overwhelmingly in the country," the Roman Catholic Church is turning to our rural areas with enthusiasm and a program to capture the country.

The burning concern of the Catholic church with agriculture arises from the altogether unique relationship which exists universally between agricultural occupations and the central institution of Christian, nay of all, civilization, namely, the family. The farm is the native habitat of the family. Industrial society works against the family and in favor of divorce, desertion, temporary unions, companionate marriage; agricultural society is characterized by the strength, permanence, and unity of the marriage bond and the comparative rarity of its dissolution.[2]

Because of a declining birth rate careful students are saying that a stationary population will be reached in the United States in the next few decades. Catholic leaders are pointing out to their people that only one city in the United States with a population of over 100,000 has enough children to maintain a stationary population without additions from the country districts and that most of the cities have only about three-fourths enough children to maintain their present population. This explains why our Catholic neighbors have declared a "rural offensive" on America.

The Catholic Church, therefore, with a well-defined purpose and program proposes to garner a harvest of thousands of Catholic members in the rural areas of America. They are building hundreds of beautiful new churches in

[2] "Agriculture and Vocation," *Christian Rural Fellowship Bulletin,* 1938.

rural America and landscaping the grounds. These churches make a strong appeal to the aesthetic tastes of the individual and the community. They seem to say to weary souls, "Come in and worship."

With wisdom and foresight they are placing in charge of these rural churches what they call "quality priests," who are trained not only in the theology and traditions of the church but in rural sociology and economics as well.

In the *Manifesto on Rural Life*, published first in 1939 and again in 1944, the chapter on "The Rural Pastorate" describes the new type of priest for rural work as follows:

The large city parish can to some extent depend on its prestige, but the standing of a little country parish depends upon the personality of the pastor. In the open country, judgment, diplomacy, activity, progressiveness and leadership are the natural virtues required of a priest. The country pastor must be a community leader. He must know rural problems. He must have sympathy with rural ideals and aspirations. He must love the country; he must know country life: the difficulties that the farmer has to face in his business, some of the great scientific revelations made in behalf of agriculture, the great industrial forces at work for the making or unmaking of the farmer, the fundamental social problems of the life of the open country.

In other words the Catholic Church proposes that the rural priest shall be as good as the best with special training for the rural field.

The country home offers a better opportunity than an urban home for the growth and cultivation of those values, habits, and characteristics so necessary for the development and perpetuity of our national life.

14

What are these values, habits, and characteristics?

One is work. In a farm home, where children are an asset and not a liability, there is work for all. According to the old saying, "All work and no play makes Jack a dull boy." It is just as true that all play and no work makes Jack a playboy. Idleness has long been recognized as the seedbed of much evil. One of the problems of the urban parent is to find useful employment for his children, employment which will occupy their minds and hands, which will develop them as useful members of society. On the farm there are fields to be plowed, harvests to be gathered, stock to be fed, cows to be milked, chores to be done. There is plenty of work on the farm for everyone, and productive work is a blessing.

Co-operation is another valuable characteristic of the country home. In a well-organized farm home each member of the family has a particular task to do and does it. Learning to co-operate in the work of the home and on the farm for the common good of the family, a boy or girl learns how to co-operate for the common good of society, the larger family.

Self-reliance may be put down as another value. The farmer is usually thought of as an individualist, and so he is. He thinks and acts for himself. Again and again he finds himself in difficult situations calling for immediate decisions. These things make him self-reliant, and self-reliance is an admirable and valuable virtue.

Thrift is another of these values. The meager income of the average farmer makes thrift and economy necessary. The farm lad is therefore likely to become a more frugal and thrifty citizen.

Respect for authority is still another quality. Farmers as a class are law-abiding citizens and teach their children respect for authority. Both the church and the state are concerned about the development of these character traits in our citizenship. They are essential characteristics for a continuing democracy.

From the church's standpoint, however, perhaps the greatest value of rural or farm life is the reverence which it produces for the supernatural. Too often the novelist has dealt only with the sordid in farm life. Too often farm life has been described as dull and humdrum. The materialistic writer of fiction has too often failed to feel or picture the thrill that comes from working with the creative processes of nature which link the worker in a co-operative effort with the Creator of earth and sea and sky. He who tills the soil is more closely associated with the miraculous and the supernatural than any other worker. Working with nature and the creative life processes from day to day, the tiller of the soil is inspired with a reverence for God that a man never gets simply in working with machines. He plows the land, he sows the seed, but he is ever conscious of his dependence upon climatic conditions, upon rain and sunshine over which he has no control, upon God, the creator and preserver of all things. His life and work become a continuing illustration of the text, "We are labourers together with God," and he comes to worship his God-partner.

Dr. Frank W. Price says:

16

The rural vocation can keep alive in us, in the men and women of our generation as of past generations, the realization of our utter dependence upon a wisdom and a power greater than our own. In labor on the land we touch the mysteries of birth and life, of death and resurrection, as nowhere else. We feel and see though we cannot explain the miracles of growth.[3]

In the operation of machines such experiences are certainly uncommon if not impossible. Machines magnify man; nature magnifies God.

A college freshman is quoted as saying, "I'm afraid I am not very religious. I just heard a sermon on prayer and am not moved to pray. I feel so much more like praying when I walk through the meadows in the morning to school." [4]

Great buildings, dams, bridges, engines, and airplanes move us to great respect for man's ingenuity and skill. But the lofty mountains, the yawning canyon, the waterfall, the starry firmament inspire us with a reverence for God.

Perhaps it is because in the rural home and open country these values are developed as nowhere else that Professor D. E. Lindstrom has called our rural population the "balance wheel" of the nation.

[3] *Christian Rural Fellowship Bulletin*, June, 1938.
[4] *Ibid.*, November, 1938.

CHAPTER II

The Church and the Land

A GOSPEL preacher is expected to minister to the "spiritual life" of his congregation. He must make converts to the Christian faith and train them in Christian character building. But he carries a wider range of responsibilities than that. He must minister to the total life of his people, and because of this fact these chapters deal with phases of service other than those ordinarily classed as evangelistic and educational. In this chapter we want to discuss the responsibility of the church and the pastor for the soil.

W. C. Lowdermilk was asked by the United States Department of Agriculture in 1938 to make a survey of land usages in England, Holland, France, Italy, North Africa, and the Near East. The war interrupted this survey, but after a year and a half of careful work he brought back to this country a story of land usages full of frightful significance.

He described his depressing travels through once prosperous areas which are now desolate and depopulated. He pictured them as the graveyards of great cities, civilizations, and flourishing cultures. He was filled with consternation as he visited great areas in North Africa, Palestine, Trans-Jordan, Syria, and other sections known in history as prosperous and productive lands, which have now lain desolate and unproductive for centuries.

Mesopotamia, which once maintained thirty to fifty million people and renowned civilizations of culture, now maintains in poverty and want only about five million people.

The land of Canaan was described by Joshua as a land flowing with milk and honey. Dr. Lowdermilk found that the soils of this once happy land have been washed off the slopes to bedrock over more than half the upland area. The denuded highlands of Judea are dotted with the ruins of abandoned town and village sites. For centuries the unleashed forces of erosion have been washing the soils of the Promised Land into the valleys to make marshes or out to sea. He brought back similar stories from China and other lands.

It was during this extended research and study that he got his inspiration for an Eleventh Commandment:

XI. Thou shalt inherit the earth as a faithful steward, conserving its resources and productivity from generation to generation. Thou shalt safeguard the fields from soil erosion, thy living waters from drying up, thy forests from desolation, and protect thy hills from overgrazing by thy herds that thy descendants may have abundance forever. If any shall fail in this stewardship of the land, thy fruitful fields shall become sterile, stony ground and wasting gullies, and thy descendants shall decrease and live in poverty or perish from off the face of the earth.

If this commandment lacks divine authority, authority may be found for it in the certain destruction which

19

awaits every nation that ignores it. Surely the time has come for emphasizing such a commandment in our own land.

Our National Resources Committee indicates that at least one half of the original fertility of the American continent has disappeared through water and wind erosion and mining the soil for crops; that three fourths of the farm lands in the United States are in the Mississippi Valley; and that previous to World War II an estimated equivalent of one farm a day vanished in the waters of that great river.

Wind erosion, though more dramatic, is less serious. Nevertheless, its destructive effect cannot safely be minimized. One unprecedented duster alone, that of May 11, 1934, carried away an estimated 300,000,000 tons of the topsoil of Nebraska, western Kansas and Oklahoma, and the bordering parts of Texas and Colorado. On the basis of 1,000 tons of topsoil to cover one acre seven inches deep, this duster took out of crop production three thousand one-hundred-acre farms.

When we realize that the soil which sustains life lies in a thin layer of an average depth of seven or eight inches over the face of the earth and that the earth beneath it is as dead and sterile as the moon, we will appreciate more fully the need of preserving the soil. If this layer of topsoil could be represented on a twenty-four-inch globe, it would be a film three millionths of one inch thick. That thin film is all that stands between man and extinction.

Perhaps it was a faint realization of this fact that led

Patrick Henry on one occasion to exclaim, "He is the greatest patriot who stops the most gullies!"

And yet here in America for the most part, either knowingly or unknowingly, these astounding facts are tragically ignored. It is now a matter of common knowledge among those who have any acquaintance with our soil conservation problems that 35,000,000 acres of land in the United States have been completely destroyed for farming purposes by water and wind erosion, that the topsoil has been partly or entirely removed from an additional 125,000,000 acres, and that 100,000,000 more acres are seriously affected. In terms of cropland alone approximately one fourth of the area now used for the production of crops has been ruined for such purposes by erosion. Some are now saying that this country may even cease to be a world power within the next one hundred years if we continue to use the land without more serious regard to intelligent soil conservation practices.

What can be accomplished by a scientific soil conservation program? C. M. Malone of the Second National Bank of Houston, Texas, reports:

In our soil conservation work we have found that if the farmers and ranchers of Texas will follow proper soil conservation methods, the farm income of this state can be increased from $500,000,000 to $1,000,000,000 per year. This sounds like a big figure, but it is possible when you realize that actual figures show that production has been increased by soil conservation methods from 30 per cent to 400 per cent.

At the experiment station at Angleton, Texas, on a pasture program where they fertilized and planted the pasture properly, the cattle increased in weight 318 pounds per head in one year; and the feed cost on the twelve heads was $64.96. On the untreated pasture adjoining, the increase in weight was 125 pounds; and the cost of feed on twelve heads was $175.67.

In east Texas we have cases where sweet potato production on untreated soil was 40 bushels per acre, while on an adjoining tract where soil conservation was practiced 188 bushels per acre were produced, or almost five times as much as on the untreated soil.

Does the church have any interest in such a program?

For years I have driven from time to time by run-down, dilapidated, unpainted country churches and found myself saying, "Why don't these congregations repair, paint, and beautify these houses of worship and make them inviting? Are they without pride or aesthetic taste?" I have not always understood, but now I feel that I have found at least a partial answer. Too often the churches are unable to make repairs and beautify.

A depleted, eroded, impoverished soil means a depleted, eroded income on the part of those who live on the land; and this low income means a depleted income and support for the churches which they attend.

The following table indicates percentages of farms with low gross farm incomes or value of farm products sold and used by farm households over a period of fifteen years.

	1929	1939	1944
Less than $1,000	46.5	66.9	38.9
Less than 600	26.7	49.6	25.6
Less than 250	6.3	20.2	9.4

While 38.9 per cent of our farm people have a gross farm income of less than $1,000 and 25.6 per cent of them an income of less than $600, we cannot reasonably expect adequate support for our country churches.

Agricultural conditions and incomes greatly improved during the World War II period, but increased costs of production and increased costs of living prevented low-income farmers from reaping the benefits they might have otherwise enjoyed, with the result that their status has not greatly changed.

It has been found that living expenditures in seven states increased from 29 to 65 per cent during World War II and that farm production expenses almost doubled between 1935 and 1944.

Recent studies by the Bureau of Human Nutrition and Home Economics of the Department of Agriculture show that in spite of wartime prosperity many families in rural areas still have low incomes. Of white families living on Tennessee farms three fifths had net money incomes of one thousand dollars or less in 1944. One fourth had incomes of five hundred dollars or less. In Laurene County, Georgia, three fourths of the families living in the open country had net money incomes of one thousand dollars or less in 1944–45. Incomes were somewhat higher in Highland County, Ohio. More than three fifths of the families living in the open country had incomes over one thousand dollars; less than one fifth had incomes of less than five hundred dollars.

Since low-income farm families are scattered widely throughout the nation, it is reasonable to assume that similar studies in other counties and states would reveal similar facts.

In 1940 for the country as a whole the median value of owner-occupied farmhouses was $1,028. For the North the median was $1,450; for the West, $1,084; but for the South it was only $600. These conditions have changed very little since that time.

Do not these facts answer the question? How can we expect people who live under such conditions and with such incomes to support adequately a church program which will meet the needs of their communities?

The church then has an economic interest in the soil. The country church has to rely largely upon those who live on the soil for its support. When their living is reduced to a marginal or submarginal existence by an eroded or wasted soil, the church must in turn expect a decreased or eroded income for the support of its program; and this decrease has resulted in the closing of thousands of country churches.

That there is a direct relation between the productivity of the soil and the church budget has been proved by T. S. Buie of the Soil Conservation Service. A few years ago he made a survey of 222 churches in South Carolina which revealed this fact.

These churches were divided into three groups, A, B, and C. Group A contained forty-seven churches in farming areas where the soil was only moderately eroded. Group B contained eighty-nine churches in farming areas where the erosion was moderate to severe. Group C contained eighty-six churches in farming areas where erosion was severe and most of the land was classed as unsuitable for cultivation.

The average church membership in these groups was:

> Group A—160 members each
> Group B—132 members each
> Group C—105 members each

The financial contributions of the respective churches to various causes were as follows:

> For the support of the pastor
> Group A—$431.37 each
> Group B— 299.93 each
> Group C— 241.09 each

> Contributions for all purposes
> Group A—$879.77 each
> Group B— 594.94 each
> Group C— 406.30 each

> Average per capita contributions
> Group A—$5.49 per member
> Group B— 4.50 per member
> Group C— 3.87 per member

From an economic standpoint then, the rural pastor needs to be interested in the question of soil conservation.

Arthur Moore says: "The right use of the earth is needed to raise the level of rural living. *It is a moral problem.*" [1] I too hold that the question of soil conservation is a moral question.

Some months ago I attended a conference on "Saving Soils and Souls." This conference was something new.

[1] Arthur Moore, *The Farmer and the Rest of Us* (Boston: Little, Brown & Co., 1945), p. 216.

From the beginning the church has been interested in saving souls, but an interest in soils was an innovation. But the time has come when the church must take a more active and intelligent interest in the redemption and saving of the soil upon which the life of every one of us depends. Men need to be taught that they are stewards of the soil as well as stewards of money, time, talent, and influence. For untold generations we have recognized our stewardship in these fields. The time has come when we must recognize our stewardship in this field also. The misuse of our soil is as much a sin as the misuse of our money. The exploitation of our land is as sinful as the wasting of our substance in riotous living. When we knowingly exploit the soil and rob it, or mine it, of its fertility, leaving it poorer and less capable of production than when we began to use it, we become thieves and robbers of those who come after us. This is why the church has a message here, a message for all who own or till the soil.

The good earth is like a bank. You may have a substantial deposit in the bank, but if you keep writing checks against your account without continually making other deposits, the time will come when your check will be turned down for insufficient funds. The good earth is like that.

When you haul two tons of alfalfa hay to market, you carry off from your farm 588 pounds of nitrogen, 97 pounds of phosphate, 194 pounds of potash, and 143 pounds of lime which have been taken from your soil.

When you haul away twenty-five bushels of corn, you

carry 135 pounds of nitrogen, 45 pounds of phosphate, 11 pounds of potash, and 35 pounds of lime.

When you take a bale of cotton to market, you carry off 246 pounds of nitrogen, 78 pounds of phosphate, 30 pounds of potash, and 6 pounds of lime.

When you haul twenty-five bushels of wheat to market, you haul off your farm 197 pounds of nitrogen, 74 pounds of phosphate, 16 pounds of potash, and 1 pound of lime.

Varying amounts are likewise removed by other crops, as shown in the table on page 29.[2]

Unless these minerals or soil constituents are restored, nature will gradually decline to honor our labor checks with good and paying crops. If we use up the mineral contents of the soil that are essential to crop production and never replace them, we become miners and robbers of the soil. If the church has a right to cry out against any crime, it surely has a right to cry out against the crimes of people against the soil, the holy earth.

The church of necessity then is interested in the soil from an economic standpoint. But the church has still another reason for being interested in the land. Jesus said, "I am come that they might have life, and that they might have it more abundantly." Has it ever occurred to you that abundant life has a very direct connection with the soil? Has it ever occurred to you that there is any connection between the quality of folks and the quality of the soil upon which they live? Modern scientific research declares there is.

[2] See Virginia A. & M. College Bulletin No. 97, revised by U. S. Dept. of Agriculture, 1938, p. 29.

Karl Mickey says: "The most serious loss resulting from erosion and soil exhaustion is not quantitative, but qualitative. It has to do with the quality of life the soil supports." [3]

Julian S. Huxley points out that soil deficient in calcium and phosphorus lacks the elements for proper bone growth of both livestock and humans. Cattle, for instance, raised exclusively on lush grasses on the Mississippi Gulf coast were lean and afflicted with osteomalacia and rickets because of lack of minerals in the soil. A cross section of their bones showed them to be honeycombed. Ranchers in that section supplement the grass with minerals to produce sound cattle.

Soils low in nitrates and other chemicals produce vegetation lacking in the proteins essential to the building and repairing of body tissues. Science declares that the same thing applies equally to humans. A baby will not have good bones if its formula is made with the milk of a cow whose feed came from soil deficient in calcium and phosphorus. And the adult will not build muscles and good red blood from the steak of a steer fed on grasses and grain from leached and eroded soils devoid of protein-building minerals and iron.

These things lay tremendous emphasis upon soil content. If we are to have a rugged, robust people, we must have a soil rich in those mineral contents necessary for the building of strong physiques. If our soil has lost these essentials through erosion, they need to be replaced. If

[3] *Man and the Soil* (Chicago: International Harvester Co., 1945).

Amount of Plant Food Removed from the Soil by Crops Expressed in Fertilizer Equivalents

Crops	Amount	16% Nitrogen (lbs.)	20% Super-phos-phate (lbs.)	50% Muriate of Potash (lbs.)	Equiva-lent Ground Lime-stone 90% (lbs.)
Alfalfa hay	2 tons	588	97	194	143
Barley	25 bus.	142	52	15	1.5
Barley straw	1200 lbs.	44	7	36	9.6
Corn	25 bus.	135	45	11	.35
Corn stover	1400 lbs.	82	15	56	16
Cotton	1 bale	246	78	30	6
Cowpea hay	2 tons	745	115	139	113
Crimson clover hay	2 tons	565	92	179	131
Lespedeza hay	2 tons	513	87	81	99
Oats	25 bus.	96	30	8	2
Oat straw	1600 lbs.	64	24	64	14
Pasture	2 tons	720	133	186	66
Peanuts	1500 lbs.	375	51	37	6
Peanut hay	2 tons	387	60	121	113
Rye	25 bus.	185	64	19	1.5
Rye straw	3000 lbs.	90	38	62	21
Soybean seed	20 bus.	443	83	55	6
Soybean hay	2 tons	593	115	79	96
Tobacco leaves	1000 lbs.	170	23	96	52
Wheat	25 bus.	197	74	16	1
Wheat straw	2250 lbs.	86	18	43	12

Virginia A. & M. College, Bulletin 97
Revised by USDA 1938.

29

they were not there to begin with, they can and need to be put into the soil.

Rural pastors should therefore be actively interested in the organization of soil conservation districts in the areas which they serve. The government will co-operate in the organization of such a district, but it has not yet attempted to force the organization upon any community. Your county agent can tell you how to proceed.

This is a part of the abundant life program of our Lord, and the church and its ministry need to emphasize our responsibility in this field. It was Jesus who said, ". . . Ye shall know the truth, and the truth shall make you free." The truth in the field of agriculture, brought to light in recent years through scientific experimentation and discovery, can help to rid our nation of poverty, fear, and disease, if only it is used in an intelligent and persistent manner.

The church, while not neglecting the souls of men, must take more interest in the soils of men which are necessary to their physical well-being. Too long the church and her ministry have followed an up-in-the-sky policy. The time has come for us to adopt a more down-to-earth policy. "Godliness is profitable unto all things, having promise of the life *that now is*, and of that which is to come."

One rural pastor writes: "My community had been burned over by revivalism until religion had been divorced from the common life of the people." Many others have had a similar feeling.

Without minimizing the importance of "revivalism,"

30

I fear that this has been true in far too many instances. Many of us in the past have been so busy trying to keep our people out of a hell-to-be that we have done little to get them out of a hell they are now in. Seeing no connection between religion and economic improvement, we have sought to comfort them with the hope of a heaven of rest and ease and plenty in the world to come. We have generated tremendous power in annual emotional revivals without much meaning to modern life. They have been too effervescent. Our country people need salvation in terms of more productive land, which means better living conditions, better health, better education, better churches, and a more abundant life here as well as hereafter. We are stewards of both soils and souls.

CHAPTER III

The Church and Community Health

A few years ago I purchased a book entitled *Roots in the Earth* by Waring and Teller. In this book I came across the statement that in 1936 nearly 250,000 rural women in this country gave birth to their babies without the benefits, care, or protection of a physician. This is amazing. This book also said that one baby in ten was born in this country that year without a doctor's care! And this occurred in Christian America!

Also several years ago a report of the United States Technical Committee on Medical Care declared that with adequate medical care 200,000 deaths a year could be prevented in this country! This means 600 needless deaths a day!

Such a situation certainly merits the serious consideration of the church and the gospel ministry.

During the course of World War II nearly five million male registrants between eighteen and thirty-seven years of age were examined and classified as unfit for military service because of physical defects. These constituted about 30 per cent of all those examined. About one third of the young women who applied for admission to the Women's Army Corps were rejected for similar reasons.

The percentage of rejections in both cases from rural areas was considerably greater than from urban areas.

Disraeli once said, "The health of the people is really the foundation upon which all their happiness and all their powers as a State depend." If this is true, both the state and the church have here a stewardship that they dare not ignore.

In May, 1945, *Better Health for Rural America*, an informing bulletin. published by the Inter Bureau Committee of the United States Department of Agriculture, stated that approximately 57,000,000 of our people are living in what are called our "rural" areas, communities of less than 2,500 population. This bulletin pointed out that the decline of our death rate has been less in the country in recent years than in the cities. In 1900 the American farmer claimed a death rate 50 per cent below that of his city cousins. Today he can claim only a 10 per cent advantage. In fact, the death rate among infants and small children is actually higher in rural areas and small towns than in large cities. Deaths from the very diseases which modern science and sanitation are best able to prevent are highest in rural areas.

The Children's Bureau of the United States Department of Labor reports that in 1943 there were 204,000 mothers in the United States who gave birth to their babies without the care of an attending physician, which is a little better record than in 1936. Of these, 160,000 were rural mothers. In Texas alone, 22,875 babies were born in 1943 without the care of a physician. Death among mothers in connection with childbirth was almost one-third higher in rural areas than in large cities. And infant mortality was over one-fourth higher.

The Farm Security Administration conducted an interesting study in seventeen states involving thousands of low-income farm people. This study showed between three and four significant defects per person. Fourteen per cent of the men and women, for example, had varicose veins. One out of every twelve farm operators had a hernia. Nineteen per cent had hemorrhoids; and in white families alone 42 per cent of the wives had internal tears due to childbirth. Many had defective vision not corrected by glasses or badly infected tonsils. There were many children underweight because of malnutrition, and serious conditions of the teeth occurred in practically every one.

On November 10, 1945, the President of the United States sent a message to Congress which declared that on an average day there are seven million people in this country who are incapacitated for work by sickness or injury. Four or five hundred million working days are lost every year because of illness and accidents, about forty times the number of days lost because of strikes during the ten years before the war.

Sick people cannot work. People in poor health are ineffective workers. These facts, therefore, indicate untold suffering and great economic loss, not only to the families involved but to the nation as a whole.

The nutritionists tell us that forty million people in the United States are suffering from faulty diets, and General Lewis B. Hershey declares that one third of all draft rejections in World War II were due directly or indirectly to deficient diets.

The National Safety Council has reported that 16,000 residents of the nation's farms were killed in accidents in 1945 and 1,500,000 others injured, the highest totals since 1942.

What can the church and the rural pastor do to help provide better medical care for rural people? More rural hospitals, health centers, public health nurses, and courses in health education are needed in almost all of the rural areas of America.

The Inter Bureau Committee points out that over 1,250 of the 3,070 counties in our nation are without a single satisfactory general hospital, and over 700 of these are counties which have populations exceeding ten thousand. Furthermore, hundreds of the counties do not even have the benefit of a single public health nurse. There were nineteen thousand public health nurses in this country in 1941, and yet only one county out of every four had one.

Hundreds of small towns and rural areas are without the doctors and dentists they need. They cannot be drafted to go to these areas. They must be attracted to them. Good doctors and dentists will be more easily secured for a community if a hospital or health center equipped to aid a physician in the practice of modern medicine is provided. Otherwise, veteran doctors and new graduates will choose to settle in the cities where adequate facilities are available. If in addition to a small hospital or health center a physician could be provided

35

with a comfortable home and guaranteed a minim
income for the first year—say of four or five thous
dollars—by agreement to make up from county tax fu
or otherwise any amount which his income from pri
practice might fall short of the guaranteed sum, n
any community could secure a competent physician

Every county should have a department of pu
health to promote farm safety, sanitation, the preven
and control of acute communicable diseases, vene
infection, tuberculosis, the care of expectant mothers
infants, the protection of children in and out of sch
and the education of its citizenship about healt
living. But in 1941 there were almost 1,400 ou
America's 3,070 counties without the service of a
time health department. Practically all of these
rural counties. And even in the counties where he
departments are functioning, many rural people
never heard of them. The departments are too c
housed in dingy corners in the basement of the c
house and because of lack of information are lo
upon as intended for poor people and not for the
munity as a whole.

Rural ministers and churches in areas needing b
hospital facilities or departments of health could,
should, take steps to secure them. Any state departr
of health will be glad to give guidance and help in
enterprises.

The government is very much interested in p
health and is paying over $700,000,000 a year for p
health services. About one fifth of this amount is

by the federal government, four fifths by the states and from local funds. The total includes expenditures for public health services, public hospitals, maternal and child health services, and services for crippled children; but it does not include the cost of medical services for the armed forces. In a number of states the departments of health are conducting experimental prepayment medical care programs. Group insurance protection can be secured by members of certain farm organizations and agencies which are promoting the interests of the small-income farmer. But as yet the government has not found a way of adequately insuring the health of the great multitude who need it most.

Industrial groups and a few other groups have access to the benefits of certain commercial prepayment medical care and hospital plans, but large groups of rural people are without such opportunity. Until the government or medical associations can find some way of bringing the benefits of modern medical science to all those who need them, we have only two solutions for caring more adequately for the health of rural people: a county health association for those who can afford to pay nominal fees for health protection or health insurance; and public help through already-established government agencies, nurses, and physicians for those who cannot financially afford to join such an association.

The rural minister can render his community or county a real service in many places by organizing or assisting in the organization of such a co-operative health association.

You will find in every county, however, a county physician whose salary is paid out of the county fund. These physicians are expected to give medical care to those who cannot otherwise afford it. A rural pastor should be intimately acquainted with his county physician and work with him in caring for the health of the disadvantaged of the county. Most county physicians will readily rely upon the judgment of an interested pastor with regard to the worthiness and need of individual cases.

When hospitalization or surgery is necessary, a rural pastor in co-operation with the county physician can secure such service in the county hospital for deserving cases, and if necessary the county will take care of all bills.

If your county does not have a county hospital, the case can be cared for in the hospital of an adjoining county, providing the county of which the patient is a resident approves and underwrites the case. The county judge is the one to see in such instances.

Where a county has no county health unit and physicians are scarce, a rural pastor can get together a few interested leaders and organize a county health association and employ a county or public health nurse, who can do much towards meeting the health needs. The schools of a county may be interested in jointly employing such a nurse. She could divide her time between the co-operating schools in caring for the health of their pupils. If the schools do not co-operate, this health association can be organized on an independent basis to

38

provide the funds and supervision necessary to secure a nurse. Your state department of health will be glad to give counsel in setting up any such enterprise.

But we have not yet exhausted all the possibilities of bringing help and information to our rural constituents. Our people can be taught to do a great many things for themselves. A rural pastor without any committee organization at all, if he has the vision and is so minded, can arrange and conduct for his people regularly a rural health institute or chautauqua. He can secure local or near-by doctors and nurses for such a program, who can discuss for his people many subjects of vital interest and concern and distribute important literature on matters of family and public health.

Let us consider for a moment poor rural sanitation. Many serious diseases come from polluted water supplies or improper facilities for disposing of human and household wastes. Two thirds of American rural families use outdoor toilets. Half of these toilets need to be repaired or completely replaced before they will be in a sanitary condition. No toilet should be located nearer than one hundred feet of any well or domestic water supply under the most favorable conditions of soil and drainage. Toilets should always be fly-tight.

A "fly catechism" by the Texas State Department of Health reveals some interesting facts. Flies are known to be the most deadly enemy of man. More people are killed by flies every year than are killed by lightning, murder, snakes, wild animals, fires, and floods combined. The common housefly is sometimes called the "typhoid fly" because it has been found to spread so much typhoid fever. This fly also spreads cholera infantum and dysentery. The fly may carry the eggs of parasitic worms and a certain form of ophthalmia. Leprosy, small-pox, plague, and tuberculosis may all be conveyed by the fly to human beings. The fly has also been found to be a carrier of polio virus but may not be the common conveyer of the disease. As many as 660,000 germs have been found on the body of a single fly!

In this connection let us consider another enemy of health and all mankind, mosquitoes. The common house mosquitoes are usually the Culex quinquefasciatus and the Aëdes aegypti, or yellow fever mosquito. An abundance of the Aëdes aegypti variety can quickly cripple a whole community with dengue fever. According to the department of health there were one million cases of dengue fever in Texas in 1922 resulting in a loss of man-hours totaling ten thousand years of time! This variety breeds only in man-made containers holding water, not in swamps or street gutters. It lays its eggs in cans, jars, tubs, old tires, barrels, vases growing ivy vines and other water plants, water barrels, cisterns, and wells.

The Anopheles quadrimaculatus, or malaria mosquito, carries on its destructive work in many parts of the country.

The world's worst mammals are rats. They carry such dread diseases as bubonic plague, typhus fever, cholera, anthrax, trichinosis, and infectious jaundice. Rats also play havoc among man's domestic animals by carrying hog cholera, swine erysipelas, fowl tuberculosis, and probably hoof-and-mouth disease. Surely these facts should interest our rural people.

The United States Public Health Service estimates that there are almost as many rats as people in the United States, or about 125,000,000 rats. Besides spreading disease each of these rats consumes nearly two dollars' worth of foodstuff a year and ruins and defiles enough food, merchandise, furniture, and other supplies to total nearly ten times that much. The total cost of one rat per year then is approximately twenty dollars. If we accept the estimate of the Public Health Service that there are 125,000,000 rats in the United States, these rats are costing us annually $2,500,000,000.

A recent news sketch in a movie declared that seventeen million people now living in the United States will die of cancer, that more people died of cancer in the United States during the period of World War II than were lost in the service during that same period.

From the literature of the American Cancer Society, Inc., 350 Fifth Avenue, New York, comes the information that approximately 175,000 Americans die of cancer every year. One out of every eight deaths in the United States is caused by this disease. It causes twice as many deaths as tuberculosis. The cancer death rate, the number of deaths per 100,000 population, has increased from 63 in 1900 to 122 in 1942. But the picture is not as dark as these facts seem to indicate. At least one third, perhaps one half, of those who die of cancer, sixty to ninety thousand a year, could be saved if they received diagnosis and treatment during the early stages of the disease.

Four million people in the United States have syphilis, one in every thirty! Over 100,000 people die from it in this country every year. And 60,000 unborn babies are infected by it. One in seven cases of blindness and one in ten cases of insanity are due to syphilis.

The most scientific and authoritative literature available on all of these health subjects and many others can be obtained free from your state departments of health and certain government agencies in Washington, D. C. for distribution in your church or community health institutes or chatauquas. Where electricity and a movie machine are available, a number of these agencies gladly furnish, either free or at very low cost, most interesting and informing pictures on many health subjects.

The rural minister has sufficient reason for interesting himself in the health problems of his people. The Master was interested in the physical needs and well-being of the people about him. Our Lord is known as the compassionate Christ. We read again and again how he was moved with compassion toward all who needed his help. He was touched by their suffering and pain. He took as his first text:

The Spirit of the Lord is upon me, because he hath anointed me to preach the gospel to the poor; he hath sent me to heal the brokenhearted, to preach deliverance to captives, and recovering of sight to the blind, to set at liberty them that are bruised.

And we read again and again how during his wonderful ministry, "he healed them," "he healed them," "he healed them!"

He healed the nobleman's son, he cured the demoniac in the synagogue, he healed the demoniac of Gadara, he cured Peter's mother-in-law of a fever, he cleansed and healed numerous lepers, he restored the palsied to normalcy, he made the lame to walk, he gave sight to the blind and hearing to the deaf and cured a man of dropsy. Through all the years we have thought of him as the great Physician. And he has commissioned his church and his disciples to heal the sick:

. . . As ye go, preach, saying, The kingdom of heaven is at hand. Heal the sick, cleanse the lepers, raise the dead. . . . Freely ye have received, freely give. (Matt. 10:7–8.)

. . . He called his twelve disciples together, and gave them power and authority over all devils, and to cure diseases. And he sent them to preach the kingdom of God, and to heal the sick. (Luke 9:1–2.)

No church or pastor can follow Jesus and turn a deaf ear to the suffering multitudes of mankind. We have been blessed as no other generation with healing knowledge. We dare not keep silence. We must lift our voices in behalf of the suffering of our land and of every land. We cannot expect the great Physician to bless and prosper us if we fail to do everything in our power to bring the blessings of modern medical science to all who need them—to mothers in the pangs of childbirth, to children being born into the world, to the poor unable to procure medical aid for themselves.

CHAPTER IV

The Church and Recreational Life

THE GOVERNMENT is very much interested in community recreation and the proper use of leisure time and is spending millions of dollars each year for recreational purposes. There are now twenty-seven national parks, two national historic parks, eleven national military parks, and numerous other smaller parks. The national park and monument system of the country now has a total of 21,000,000 acres and reports upwards of 16,000,000 visits a year. It has been estimated that between 1932 and 1937 the expenditures of the federal government for recreational facilities and leadership totaled $1,500,000,000. The number of municipal recreation buildings quadrupled in the period 1925–35. In 1938 a total of over $60,000,000 in local and federal funds was spent for recreation in communities having municipally supported programs.

There are 1,600 state parks, forests, parkways, historic sites, and other recreational areas established and controlled by state agencies. These areas contain some 6,000,000 acres.

These facts indicate something of the value which the government is placing upon the recreational life of its people. We learned during the war the need of planning the recreational life of our people as thoroughly and scientifically as education, health, and all other elements of public welfare are planned. Local leaders everywhere are now convinced that our community building efforts should include planning recreational facilities for our present and future populations.

But rural communities have lagged far behind urban centers in providing recreational facilities for their people, and rural youth particularly are lacking in social and recreational opportunities. The church has provided them with practically no such advantages. Out-of-school youth and youth from low-income families stand in greatest need. Girls constitute the largest group of recreationally underprivileged youth, while youth in their late teens are the forgotten youth of our country.

Our homes too have failed to provide recreational opportunities.

A study in a rural county in New York State reported that the proportion of youth whose "families do not provide facilities or consciously try to carry on 'sociability' activities for the family group," was 87 per cent.[1]

Surely we have neglected here a great opportunity for Christian service. Recreation develops character, the kind of character depending upon whether the recreation is moral or immoral. Desirable civic qualities are also fostered by recreation. Children and adults alike learn to respect the rights of others in play and "discover the meaning of freedom through co-operative action."

[1] C. Gilbert Wrenn and D. L. Harley, *Time On Their Hands* (Washington, D. C.: American Council on Education, 1941), Chapter I.

The crime record of the nation continues to climb at an alarming rate. The Federal Bureau of Investigation reports for 1945 indicate increases in crime more pronounced and widespread throughout the country than have been recorded in many years. A substantial upswing in crime was registered for cities of all sizes in each of the nine geographical divisions of the nation. All classes of crime show a decided increase over the estimated totals of 1944. A substantial number of the major crimes were committed by young people under voting age, seventeen standing out as the predominating age among arrested persons, with eighteen second. The over-all increase of 1945 over 1944 amounted to 12.4 per cent rise in the cities and 8.5 per cent rise in the rural areas. The record of murders, robberies, and rape showed an increase in rural communities over the cities. Some rural agencies listed very few crimes, and it is likely that some reports were based on records of arrest rather than on records of offenses reported to rural law-enforcement agencies. If this is true, these reports are quite conservative.

These figures emphasize the importance of more carefully planned recreational opportunities and activities both in the city and in the country, for it is generally recognized that unsupervised leisure time is a breeder of mischief and crime. Young people left to find entertainment in taverns, cheap night clubs, unchaperoned dance halls, and domino and pool halls are sure to find encouragement in wrongdoing in these places. Crime and youthful delinquency are held in check and often prevented by recreational programs and activities.

The chief of police in Cleveland, Ohio, a few years ago declared that most of the crime in that city was committed by young men during their leisure hours. It was when they had nothing particular to do that their crimes were thought out.

William J. Cooper, United States Commissioner of Education, speaking before the law students of Chattanooga University some years ago insisted that our schools should teach the proper use of leisure time as a certain "remedy for crime."

Judge Lindsey once said, "Church prevention is wiser than court cure."

It is very difficult for some to realize that we are living in a new day. An amusing incident occurred in Missouri some years ago. The authorities of the state university secured the introduction of a bill in the legislature asking for an appropriation of $100,000 with which to construct and equip a gymnasium. Most of the legislators had grown up in a day when there was plenty of work for everybody about the house. They could see no need for gymnasiums, for volleyball courts, for athletic fields. They laughed at the idea. "Why can't these boys saw wood for exercise as we did?" they asked. The bill was defeated. But at the next meeting of the legislature representatives of the university introduced a bill asking for $200,000 for the construction and equipment of a building for the sawing of wood. They explained that the wood would have to be shipped a considerable distance and that hand-saws and labor would require an extensive plant for

47

sawing wood by so many students. The legislature voted $100,000 for a new gymnasium!

But the church too has been slow to recognize the importance of play and recreation in the life of its people. The *Discipline* of the Methodist Church in 1792 outlined the policy of Cokesbury College toward leisure:

. . . We prohibit play in the strongest terms. . . . The students shall rise at five o'clock . . . summer and winter. . . . Their recreations shall be gardening, walking, riding, and bathing, without doors; and the carpenter's, joiner's, cabinet-maker's or turner's business, within doors. . . . A person skilled in gardening shall be appointed to overlook the students . . . in that recreation. . . . A master . . . shall always be present at the time of bathing. Only one shall bathe at a time; and no one shall remain in the water above a minute. No student shall be allowed to bathe in the river. . . . The students shall be indulged with nothing that the world calls *play*. Let this rule be observed with strictest nicety; for those who play when they are young, will play when they are old.

The church has come a long way since that day, but there are many in our churches who have not yet caught up with the day in which we live.

Some time ago a class of boys staged a rebellion in their church school. They occupied a back pew in the church; and when the classes were asked to "take their places," these boys refused to budge. When the superintendent came to inquire what the trouble was, he was quickly told that they wanted a man teacher. They had had two women teachers, and one of them had been the pastor's wife. The pastor's wife had said it was a sin to play ball. The pastor, too, was opposed to dragging such worldly elements into the church. But the rebels won. They got a man teacher. And when he moved away a little later, they got another, an even younger man teacher who had his own ideas about how to manage teen-age boys. Upon his suggestion they named the class "Koah," a Hebrew word meaning strength. Their purpose was strength of body, mind, and spirit. A baseball team and a basketball team were organized. A class emblem, whistle, response, handgrip, and password were adopted. The official board refused to allow the boys the churchyard for their games or a classroom for their club meetings. They regarded the boys as a bunch of roughnecks. But the teacher had the grace and the grit to stick. When it was suggested that they go to another church, he said, "No, fellows, this is our church, and we are going to stick by her." And they did. The pastor moved in a few years and was succeeded by a more progressive and understanding minister. The class prospered. Members of that class, having grown to manhood, have since taken their places on the official board, in the choir, and as workers in the church school.

We have here the illustration of a young man, a layman, who had to win out against his pastor and his church with a group of rebel boys before a play program could be regarded as an integral part of a church program. And this is not an isolated case. Even yet in both city and country there are those who look upon work as sacred and upon play as sinful, but play is both natural and inevitable. Our young people are going to mix and mingle and play, either under the auspices of the church or otherwise.

But many of our adults also need social and recreational opportunities. People are working under greater strain and tension than ever before. This strain needs to be relieved, or disastrous results are inevitable. This is why doctors often prescribe rest and recreation for adult patients as their only need.

Multitudes of men and women exist under such conditions as to make it physically and mentally impossible for them to respond to the gospel message of the abundant life unless that gospel message comes to them in the form of opportunities for recreation as well as in the form of a challenge for self-sacrificing service. The ministry of the modern church must include a ministry of healing through play. Nor is this merely a challenge to increased efficiency in doing the world's work. There is need of creating conditions in which people can retain the hope, the faith, and love which was theirs before they were caught in the mesh of the modern world's work and care.[2]

Furthermore, guided recreational activities promote community solidarity. They afford a common ground where differences may be forgotten in the joy of participation and achievement. Representatives of all vocations and social strata of life often participate in the same recreational program, frequently resulting in the disappearance of community feuds.

If the government is interested in recreational programs for health reasons, for character building and crime

[2] Norman E. Richardson, *The Church at Play* (New York: Abingdon Press, 1922), p. 43.

prevention reasons, for democratic reasons, then surely the churches should be interested in recreational opportunities and facilities for their respective communities. We have ministers of preaching, ministers of education, ministers of music in nearly all of our large churches. The time has come for the church to recognize a ministry of play and have in every church both large and small a paid or volunteer minister of recreation.

Few churches can afford a paid minister of recreation, but almost every church can find someone who has gifts and graces for social and recreational leadership. Physical education is being taught in nearly all our schools. One who has had such training might easily qualify as a volunteer director or minister of recreational life in the church. Such a position should carry the same honor and dignity as a church-school superintendent, or church-school teacher, or the presidency of the Woman's Society, or a place on the official board. Such leadership is just as necessary and just as religious. We need to broaden our ministry at this point as well as at some other points. Rural people crave fellowship and social intercourse as well as city people. They must learn how to live as well as how to make a living. Our people have been so busy pioneering that many of them have not yet learned how to play and live. They need to be taught. Other organizations are recognizing play as a primary need. The church must. Surely we cannot be very proud of the fact that most of what has been done for rural youth in the way of recreation has been done by agencies other than the church.

Shorter working hours have created much more leisure time in the city than in rural areas, and this accounts for the attention which has been given to public recreation in our larger towns and cities. But rural people also find that they have more leisure time on their hands than ever before. Modern machinery of all kinds, butane and natural gas for heating and cooking, and electricity for washing, ironing, and milking have greatly increased the leisure time of our rural people. The use of this time in the city and rural areas will largely determine the kind of country we shall have, even our national destiny.

What do we mean by recreation? The definition given by Superintendent William Maxwell of New York City years ago is still good today.

The word recreation as applied to this activity (community centers) means far more than amusement. While the play spirit is pre-eminent in every center, fun is only a segment of the circle. To give occupation to the idle, entertainment to the weary, and training for future citizenship by developing the body, the mind, and the heart, is really creating a new life, and this is the aim and purpose of a recreation center.[3]

And I may add, the purpose of every intelligent recreational program.

If a recreational program can be used to promote better health, to train people in the democratic way of life, to prevent crime and juvenile delinquency, to build Christian character, what can the rural pastor do in behalf of such a program?

He can encourage securing rural parks and playgrounds

[3] Wrenn and Harley, op. cit., p. 71.

52

which can be controlled by the moral and Christian leadership of the community. He can perhaps interest other community leaders and ministers in building a community recreational hall to be controlled by an inter-church board.

How often churches fail to do anything for the social and recreational life of their community and yet complain bitterly when dance halls, pool rooms, and domino parlors are opened up, not in the interest of wholesome recreation but for the profit which may be realized from them.

Why not offset the influence of commercialized and otherwise questionable places of entertainment and recreation by building in the community a church-controlled recreational center or pleasure-inn?

If an interchurch-controlled recreational hall is impractical and your church is without recreational facilities which it might offer to the community for such use, perhaps the school gymnasium may be secured at stated intervals for interchurch sponsored social and recreational activities. This is being done in many communities.

Public-school authorities are increasingly accepting the principle of using the schools as neighborhood recreational centers, and many communities have already voted generous bond issues for postwar school construction based on this principle. Why should not a school gymnasium or other equipment be used by a community for a wholesome recreational program? Have they not been provided by tax money? Who owns the school building? The people. They had the authority to build it. They have the authority to dispose of it. Surely they should have the right to use it for a good purpose so long as they do not interfere with the school using it.

When none of these facilities are available, the recreational program of the church or community will have to be planned for the out-of-doors on church or home lawns and in the homes of such people as may be willing to cooperate. The home that opens its doors to the young people of the church or community for an evening of play and fun may be rendering the future a larger service than the home that is willing to open its doors only to a prayer meeting for older folk.

The initiation of a recreational program in the church or circuit calls for the appointment or election of a committee on recreational activities. This committee should seek to provide recreational activity for every age group. In reasonably large classes and fellowship groups recreational committees or leaders are usually provided, but in the average small town or circuit church a committee of three might serve for the whole church.

To be successful the committee should be composed of a representative from each division: the children's division, the young people's division, and the adult division; and it should be a part of the permanent organization of the church. But in some situations the responsibility for the recreational program may have to be placed in the hands of some individual interested and qualified to lead in this field of service. There may be places and times when the pastor himself will have to become the recreational leader of his people. Any pastor with a little study, determination, and appreciation of the ministry of play can become a fairly good recreational director.

The National Recreation Association states its purpose thus:

"That every child in America shall have a chance to play. That everybody in America, young and old, shall have the opportunity to find the best and most satisfying use of leisure time." [4]

This ought likewise to be one of the objectives of the church and rural pastor. I know a pastor in a great city church today who is unable to seat his Sunday night crowds. It is not an unusual thing for hundreds of people to be turned away from his services. Most of them are young people. Young people from every denomination are flocking to his church. Why? Because of the social and recreational program his church is sponsoring. He is always present on these occasions. He is a good entertainer himself and enters enthusiastically into the play life of his young people. Such leadership will win in the country as it wins in the city. Let the rural pastor learn how to play and lead others in play, and he will do more to revive and popularize his church than anything else he can do.

We cannot discuss here in detail a recreational program for your church. If, however, you are interested in the organization of the social and recreational life of your church, I suggest that you secure a few good books on the subject and read them carefully before under-

[4] George D. Butler, *Introduction to Community Recreation* (New York: McGraw-Hill Book Co., 1940), p. 75.

taking such a program. Any publishing house will give you titles of books on games, plays, and other social activities.

But here again the initiation of such a program will depend upon an awakened interest on the part of the pastor in this type of ministry. A course in recreation and the wise and proper use of leisure time would prove more valuable to many ministers than just another course in Bible. Having learned how to play and having learned how to use leisure time as an asset in the development of Christian character, a minister can teach his people how to play and use their leisure time most advantageously for social, physical, and spiritual ends.

Our adults are awaiting leadership, and eleven million young people in the villages and on the farms are looking to the rural pastors of America for guidance in this field of service. Such leadership will help to bring to our people a happier and more abundant life.

CHAPTER V

The Church and Community Agencies

MORTGAGED farm ownership and tenancy are problems which the rural church must face. In 1910 the farm mortgage indebtedness of this country amounted to $3,207,863. By 1920 it had increased to $8,448,772. This indebtedness reached its peak in 1930 when it totaled $9,630,768. Between 1910 and 1935 approximately 600,-000 farmers unable to pay their taxes and meet their mortgage obligations lost their farms.

By 1941 the total farm mortgage indebtedness of the country had been reduced to $6,534,487. By January, 1946, it was down to $5,080,717. This reduction was made possible by increased production and high war prices. This means that the farm mortgage indebtedness was approximately $3,368,055 less at the close of World War II than it was at the close of World War I.

But according to the Department of Agriculture there were more mortgaged farms in this country in 1940 than in 1935 and almost as many as in 1930. Mortgaged farms represented 38.8 per cent of the total farms in the United States in 1940, as compared with 34.5 per cent in 1935 and 40.1 per cent in 1930. While the farmer found himself in a better economic state at the close of World War

II than at the close of World War I, mortgaged farm ownership continues as a major problem.

The government is anxious to help the farmers own their farms—to make it possible for ambitious, hard working tenants and sharecroppers to secure farms of their own—and has established a number of agencies to assist them in this direction.

The Farm Credit Administration as an agency of the United States Department of Agriculture provides generous assistance for worthy and capable people who need help in purchasing land or in retiring the indebtedness on their farms and ranches or in improving them. This agency carries on its work through various departments. Dismissing detailed organization of this agency, let us consider the help available through the Federal Land Bank and the Production Credit Association.

The Federal Land Bank makes loans through a local Farm Loan Association for purchasing farm or ranch land, for refinancing agricultural debts, or for making improvements. A loan on a homestead may be obtained to construct or repair buildings or make most any kind of improvements. These loans bear 4 per cent interest and are made to mature in from twenty to thirty-four years. The interest rate on these loans can never be raised after the contract has been closed. Payments on the loan are made every six months. Loans range from one hundred to fifty thousand dollars but can never exceed 65 per cent of the appraised normal agricultural value of the farm or ranch.

Production Credit Associations operating under the

Farm Credit Administration make loans for all purposes in connection with farm and ranch operations. One loan may include the direct expenses of production—the purchase of livestock, feed, fertilizer, fuel, grease for the tractor, tires for tractor and truck, machinery or repair parts, and pay for hired labor—and the payment of debts, life insurance premiums, land loan installments, and taxes. The loans are made for the period of time necessary to produce the crops or livestock with which to make the repayment. These loans do not ordinarily run for more than twelve months, but if credit conditions warrant, they may be renewed.

The Farm Security Administration is an agency set up by the United States Department of Agriculture to help disadvantaged small farmers make an economic and social recovery. Farm ownership loans are available through this agency to tenants, sharecroppers, and farm laborers for the purchase of farms. The program has been very greatly liberalized to include World War II veterans. Under this plan the total purchase price of the farm may be borrowed, but this amount can in no case exceed twelve thousand dollars. A period of forty years is allowed for the repayment of a farm purchase loan, but the loan may be paid off as rapidly as the borrower is capable of doing so. These loans bear only 3.5 per cent interest.

Rehabilitation loans are also available for the purchase of machinery, livestock, feed, fencing, pressure cookers, and other farm and home essentials, even including necessary operation expenses. Loans can also be secured for the installation of water facilities.

Co-operating loans are now enabling seventeen thousand groups of farmers to own and use jointly farm machinery, purebred sires, and processing plants. Local medical care plans set up with the co-operation of the organized medical profession make possible health protection not ordinarily enjoyed by disadvantaged people. Other services of the Farm Security Administration include tenure improvement and help in providing better sanitation for the farm home.

The Production and Marketing Administration of the federal government is the successor of the Agricultural Adjustment Administration, commonly referred to as the AAA. This new agency has a representative in every county. In addition to marketing quotas and farm acreage allotments, which are perhaps best known, the Production Marketing Association has a soil conservation program which does not conflict with any other agency of the Department of Agriculture. The agency extends financial grants to farmers and ranchers who carry out approved conservation measures on their farm and ranch units. It grants financial assistance for the construction of terrace systems and earthen dams for impounding water for livestock; drilling of wells for the sole purpose of furnishing water for livestock; eradication of noxious pasture plants; application of superphosphate, lime, and agricultural sulphur to certain crops and under certain conditions; contour farming of row crops and contour seeding of small grains; seeding of inoculated winter legumes for the purpose of adding nitrates to the soil; using green manure and cover crops, and many other conservation measures. These loans bear 3 per cent interest.

This agency also provides commodity loans to producers protecting them against low markets. These loans establish a floor for the prices a farmer receives for basic agricultural products. It also provides a crop insurance program which, for a stated premium, protects wheat and cotton farmers against loss of crops due to insurable hazards.

The Farmers' Home Administration, a new agency, has recently taken over the responsibilities of the Emergency Crop and Feed Loan section of the Farm Credit Administration. The Farmers' Home Administration now makes loans to farmers who are unable to secure loans from banks or other sources. Loans are also made to finance the purchase or production of feed for livestock. The maximum loan to an individual is $3,500.

Local representatives of these various agencies are found in most counties. Your county agent can tell you where to find them.

The church, too, is becoming alarmed over the loss of so many farm homes and the inability of tenants, sharecroppers, and young people to purchase and establish themselves in homes of their own. In this connection it has been suggested that the church itself might help to build stronger rural parishes by aiding worthy young people, tenants, sharecroppers, and farm laborers in securing and establishing their homes upon the land. Many denominations have hundreds of thousands of dollars, perhaps millions of dollars, in endowments, bonds, and city mortgages. A certain element of risk is involved in all of these loans. Why not take the same risks on farm loans and help worthy young people or families to get established on the land? The same legal acumen which passes on the validity and safety of an urban loan could pass on that of a rural loan. You can never have strong churches either in the city or in the country except where the people own their own homes.

Some churches are now helping their constituents in this direction. The Mennonites in Kansas have large churches in the open country which often have memberships of one thousand and attendances of eight hundred at their worship services. The reason for this is that they have followed a colonization policy.

Roman Catholic leaders are encouraging colonization in the South and Middle West. Carefully selected families who love the land and have an aptitude for farm life are helped with long-term, low-interest loans to secure farm homes on good land. These leaders encourage individuals and groups who have money to invest to assist worthy families in acquiring family farms as a special service in the interest of the church.

The General Mission Board of the Church of the Brethren, believing in the importance of the family farm home as a national and church asset, has a policy of lending funds to those of their own faith who wish to establish farm homes. To qualify for a parish loan a couple must be faithful church workers and have some experience in farming. The farm must be so priced that it can be paid for on the basis of its long-time earning capacity. Loans range from twenty to thirty years and bear 3 per cent interest. Under favorable circumstances credit is extended up to 90 per cent of the purchase price of the farm. Through this method a rural community is built up of the same faith, and a strong rural church becomes a reality.

The Church of Jesus Christ of Latter-day Saints has long been known for the help it gives its members in times of economic distress. Between 1936 and the end of 1945 the church made 247 modest loans averaging a little under $560 at 3 per cent interest to assist members in the purchase of homes, to prevent business failures, to replace fire losses, to meet emergencies due to accidents and death, to provide necessities during times of unemployment and emergency conditions arising from other unusual circumstances. Of these loans 199 have been paid in full. Bad loans which have been written off amount to less than one third of the interest paid.

The church has also financed larger projects. An 830-acre tract of land near Boise, Idaho, was purchased and divided into sixteen units, each capable through proper management and operation of sustaining a family. These units were resold to worthy members of the church, the purchasers making down payments of 10 per cent of the purchase price. This project was started in 1941. Today eleven of the sixteen purchasers have fully paid for their land.

Another tract of 3,700 acres has been purchased by the church and divided into twenty-one units. Members purchasing these farms were without funds or equipment.

Since then they have built homes for themselves, brought the land under cultivation, made substantial payments to the church on their purchase price, and will in the near future own their homes free and clear of encumbrances.

In 1940 the church bought a defunct irrigation project in Nevada where a number of its members were about to lose their homes. The land occupied by members of the church was resold to them and payments therefor on a long term basis were arranged. All the money advanced by the church has been repaid. What these churches have done, and are doing, other churches might do.

More than one third of the people living in the country are tenants who have little sense of security. Living in poverty, most of them upon a very meager income, they have little or nothing with which to support the church.

Rural pastors should be acquainted with the agencies of the government and all other agencies operating in the community which have been created to give independence and a higher standard of living to rural people that they may give counsel in an hour of need to young people and other worthy families who want to establish homes in the country, for industry will likely never again be able to absorb the surplus man power of the nation. But the church should also provide means of helping in this direction. The future of the rural church is tied up with this whole question of farm home ownership.

The county agent is the local representative of the extension service of the United States Department of Agriculture. His responsibility is to serve all the farmers of his area. He is especially trained in an agricultural college and periodically called in for refresher courses. In some states he is called the farm adviser. He is always available for consultation on farm problems and should be consulted freely about crops, fertilizers, animal husbandry, and land practices.

The county home demonstration agent works with rural as well as urban families to improve home living conditions by striving for better and more convenient homes and a happier family life. The home demonstration agent gives counsel on producing more and better food for the family and on clothing construction problems.

I know of a county in which there are nineteen home demonstration clubs that have two demonstration meetings each month, working under the supervision of the county home demonstration agent. This year each home demonstration club has a food supply demonstrator and a clothing demonstrator. There are seventeen kitchen demonstrators in the county. A demonstration on one of these phases of work is given at each club meeting. The results in the homes of the people are a more balanced diet, better cooking, better sewing, more comfort, and better health for the entire household. The agents are diligent in their co-operation with other agencies to put on a better community and family life program.

Projects of individual women vary. During 1945 one woman was interested in making hats and bags. After seeing a demonstration in this type of work, she began making them for sale. During the year she made and sold ninety-seven sets and now has more orders on hand than she will be able to fill for some time. Another became interested in sewing for her neighbors. During 1945 she made 195 garments for her family and others, besides doing her housework, raising baby chicks and a garden, and canning for the family. The sewing which she did for the neighbors netted her $143.05.

Rural pastors by emphasizing the importance of using the county agent and the county home demonstration agent can help to raise the standard of living in many rural communities.

Every small town and circuit pastor should be interested in Four-H club work. The Four-H club movement was organized by the United States Department of Agriculture in connection with state colleges of agriculture and county extension organizations. It is an organization for rural boys and girls. These clubs are usually organized and conducted under the immediate supervision of county agents. Each club member does a piece of work which will demonstrate or teach better methods in homemaking or agriculture. The work is based not only on the needs and interests of the members but also on the needs of the agricultural community to which they belong. Boys and girls between ten and twenty years of age may become members.

Eminent Yale University psychologists have recently declared that the Four-H club is one of the greatest character building agencies in the United States, inasmuch as in meeting actual life situations on the farm, in the home, the school, or the community, it guides young people in making important and far-reaching decisions which build character through the formation of good habits in thinking and acting.

Because of these values rural pastors will do well to encourage their boys and girls to join Four-H clubs and to co-operate in the work of this organization.

The Future Farmers of America is a national organization of and for farm boys. The program includes studying vocational agriculture in public secondary schools which operate under the provisions of the National Vocational Act. High-school departments of vocational agriculture provide four-year courses of systematic instruction in agriculture and farm mechanics taught by teachers who are agricultural college graduates employed on a twelve months' basis. These teachers follow up their instruction throughout the year by supervising the farming operations of the students on their farms.

The primary aim of the organization is the development of agricultural leadership, co-operation, citizenship, and patriotism. Other purposes include strengthening the confidence of farm boys and young men in themselves and their work, helping them to choose intelligently their farming occupations, creating and nurturing a love for country life, improving the rural home and its surroundings, and providing organized recreational activities for rural people.

A rural pastor needs to familiarize himself with the work of this organization, to encourage its organization in communities where it is possible and yet does not exist, and to associate himself with the boys who belong to it.

The Boy Scouts of America is one of the largest youth organizations in America, having a membership of 1,500,000. The Girl Scouts have a very similar organization, though not affiliated with the Boy Scouts. There are five thousand local Girl Scout troops in America with a membership of over 500,000 girls. The Camp Fire Girls have thirteen thousand local groups, or "Campfires," in the United States and a membership of over 274,000 girls. These organizations are universally recognized as great character builders.

Rural pastors and church leaders should also interest themselves in the government's program of rural electrification.

"I am sixty-two years old and my husband is seventy. Life is just beginning for us." This is the way a Pennsylvania farm woman put it when electricity came to her farm.

Electricity can mean more to the farm and the farm home than anything else yet discovered. It means a better lighted home and lighted barns and barnyards. It makes possible an electric range, heater, iron, sewing machine, churn, sweeper, dishwasher, refrigerator, freezing unit, radio. It means an air-conditioned home. It means milking machines, lights for higher seasonable production in hen houses, chicks and pigs brooded safely, larger broods and litters. It means calves saved that would have died by lantern light, plants brought from seedlings earlier in hotbeds. It means power for running machinery in the workshop, for grinding grain and cutting ensilage, for water pumps, for irrigation. There are three hundred known uses for electricity on the farm and in the farm home!

In 1935, the year the Rural Electrification Administration program was initiated, only about 11 per cent of the farmers had electricity; and this kind of living was only a vague dream. But in 1940 approximately 25 per cent of our farmers had electricity. Nearly 25,000 additional consumers per month, or 300,000 per year, are now getting electric service under the Rural Electrification Program. Rural pastors concerned with abundant living for their people should interest themselves in bringing this service to their communities.

There are over three thousand counties in the United States, but only four hundred of these, scattered over thirty-nine states, have either county or regional library facilities. There are 39,000,000 rural people in the United States who do not have easy access to permanent library service. If a county or regional library is desired, those interested should seek counsel from their state library extension agency which takes the lead in library development in the state. Whatever its particular form, it is an official, state supported agency charged with the responsibility of developing adequate, local, public library services for every citizen. This agency is the first place to turn for help in library establishment or in improving existing facilities.

The American Library Association, 520 North Michigan Avenue, Chicago, Illinois, will give general advice and information on library establishment, desirable types of rural library service, and state aid. It works with the state library agencies, but in states without them it gives more specific advice.

But books are needed immediately in many communities which cannot wait for the establishment of a county library. The state library agency will bridge this gap by lending a collection of books to communities, schools, rural churches, and a few books at a time by mail directly to individuals.

In some states traveling libraries consisting of fifty books are sent free of all charge except the cost of transportation. These libraries are made up of the best popular books for adults and children. They are intended for rural communities and small villages which are without library facilities and are changed every three months.

What finer service can a rural pastor or church render a community without library facilities than to accept responsibility for one of these traveling libraries, caring for it and circulating the books?

Many people have really very little knowledge of the extended effort the government is making to serve its rural citizenship. For this reason our rural pastors should be acquainted with these sources of help and should encourage their constituencies to use them.

The rural pastor who learns to guide his people in the use of these agencies and organizations will lift the economic and cultural levels of his community, command respect as a community leader, and prepare the way for a stronger and better rural church.

CHAPTER VI

Ways of Serving the Rural Community

NUMEROUS communities in many sections of our land, divided into such small denominational groups that no group was able to support a competent or full-time minister, each one struggling for supremacy and recognition in the religious life of the community, have become so disgusted and disheartened with their divisions that they have sought relief through the organization of their religious life in what we now call the Larger Parish.

Through such organizations they have been able to secure more competent ministers, attract educational, musical, and recreational leaders, and unify their community religious life. What may be accomplished through a Larger Parish organization can be illustrated by what has actually been accomplished in certain communities.

The Otsquago Valley Larger Parish at Van Hornersville, New York, is an interesting study in Larger Parish pioneering. The consolidation of twenty-two districts of one-room schools into the Van Hornersville Central School with a faculty of twenty-three well-trained teachers led to the consideration of a co-operative effort on the part of the seven Protestant churches in the area to avoid "unpleasant competition." The boundaries of the parish are approximately the same as those of the consolidated school district.

This area contains 175 square miles and had a population in 1942 of 1,393, about one half the population a century before. Three villages—Van Hornersville with a population of 125 and two other small villages—are included in the area. A survey disclosed that only 12 per cent of the young people under eighteen years of age were enrolled in the church school and that scarcely a third of this number attended on Sunday.

After careful study and planning the Larger Parish was organized. A parish council was formed consisting of the staff and three representatives from each of the co-operating churches, one of the lay members in each church's representation being a young person under twenty-five years of age. Margaret J. Harris was employed as Director of Religious Education for the parish at a salary of thirteen hundred dollars with mileage allowance of an additional two hundred dollars. The Methodist, Baptist, and Universalist Mission Boards contributed five hundred dollars each to this enterprise, and the parish raised another two hundred dollars for program supplies.

One of the first accomplishments of this Larger Parish organization was to put the Bible back into the classrooms of the public school. The plan provided for a half-hour class for each group every week of the school year from the kindergarten through the junior high school. The study of the Bible in the classrooms inspired higher respect for others, reverence and respect for God, appreciation of beauty, honesty, truthfulness, helpfulness, dependability, unselfishness, and courage. It greatly reduced the number of behaviour problems and greatly decreased the use of profanity among the students.

There were three well-established church schools at the beginning of the Larger Parish program, and another was soon organized. Better transportation plans were arranged to take the children to and from church. A teacher-training class was offered in night school. The pupils in the church school met for one-half hour of study before or after the church service, and most of them attended church service. Vacation church schools and local summer camps were also arranged. Scores of young people and children accepted Christ as their Saviour during these camping periods. Easter sunrise services and other special services were arranged for the boys and girls of the whole area from time to time.

The Larger Parish program had its benefits for adults as well as for children and young people. At the beginning of the year the churches observed the Week of Prayer, and it became a school of prayer for those attending. The World Day of Prayer was observed in homes and villages rather than in one unified service. Larger Parish Thanksgiving services were held, for which either the community choral club or the combined choirs furnished the music. A traveling library and a community calendar were sponsored by the parish council. Through the efforts of the parish council the whole area was bound together in a friendly, brotherly, more nearly perfect Christian community.

Denominational ties were not disturbed or necessarily

weakened as plans were made locally and carefully adapted to the interests of the co-operating churches. Instead of the four nonresident ministers who were serving the churches in the area in 1937, there are now two full-time resident ministers who concentrate upon the needs of two churches each, located in two population centers of the Larger Parish. By this improved plan of leadership religious interests have been conserved and united in the area already defined by the centralized school program.

The Mount Desert Larger Parish of Northeast Harbor, Maine, is now in its twentieth year. Leigh Mitchell Hodges after visiting this parish wrote:

This is an interesting experiment in allied Christianity, which is worth knowing about, especially at a time when so much depends upon the unity of all forces that stand for free and decent ways. And when the church as a whole must do its best.[1]

While the Mount Desert Larger Parish was conceived as a means of relieving the economic plight of the eight Protestant churches within the area of what now constitutes the parish, Hodges points out:

The higher purpose is now the preservation of the spiritual and moral power that flows from such springheads of worship and the extension of their social benefits through a mutual sidetracking of minor doctrinal differences that have little to do with basic Christianity.

At the time of the organization of the Larger Parish, Hodges says, only one or two of the churches serving in

[1] L. M. Hodges, *A Church Co-op That Works.*

74

this area were "going concerns"; and more than 80 per cent of the residents of the area belonged to no church, not because they did not believe in religion or the church, but because they did not believe in them as they were doing business.

The churches of this area, as Hodges puts it, "buried their minor differences of belief in order to extend the major benefits of what Christ taught as essential."

So a Larger Parish was organized with a supervising council composed of two members from each church, with six others chosen from the parish at large. The parish staff includes the copastors and a director of religious education. All offerings and contributions go into a common treasury.

The combined membership of the five co-operating churches in this parish was only 173 at the time they joined the Larger Parish, and not more than a third of the children in the area attended church school. Since the organization of the Larger Parish 345 more have been added to the membership of the churches. While other rural churches have been growing smaller, the membership of the churches in this parish has more than doubled.

The Bible has been put into the public schools as a regular part of the curriculum in all the grades. A large majority of the children take the Bible courses. These give the children and young people a right feeling that religion is as necessary as arithmetic or geography.

Other social and community activities which never could have been achieved otherwise have become possible as a result of this co-operative effort on the part of "allied Christianity." As one woman put it, "It just seemed as if religion had broken through Sunday and come right into our homes."

The Larger Parish movement is growing rapidly, especially in the North and East, and scores of illustrations similar to these might be cited.

Where you cannot set up a Larger Parish, you may organize a Community Council to good advantage. Few small communities have any over-all organization to bind them together in a co-operative effort for the good of all. The churches and other groups which share responsibility for the betterment and uplift of a community might be bound together in a Community Council for such a purpose without the abandonment or the loss of identity of any church or organization. They would simply be associated together by voluntary agreement for the promotion of the common interests of the community.

Such a council may be made up of one representative of each live, active, public-interested organization of the community—the chamber of commerce, the parent-teachers association, the garden club, the Rotary Club, farm organizations, labor council—and each church in the community. In addition a few carefully selected public-interested citizens might be given membership.

The council should concern itself with the economic, religious, and cultural possibilities of the community. It can promote better schools, a community library, a community recreational program, village and community beautification, better community sanitation, a co-operative health center, and better relations between the churches themselves.

One of the functions of a Community Council is to work out a community calendar. The calendar is a list of all major events that take place during a month or year. This is a great aid in avoiding conflicts and in promoting a spirit of co-operation and understanding between the agencies at work in a community. This calendar should be worked out well in advance.

The council should hold open meetings with carefully prepared programs on subjects of interest to the community at least monthly, and a spirit of co-operation and good will should always undergird all the activities. Why should rural churches and pastors not offer leadership in such a worth-while enterprise?

Larger Parish organizations or Community Councils may be impossible in many localities. In such cases other ways of denominational procedure in caring for rural responsibilities should be investigated.

A new rural strategy is being put into operation by the Home Division of the Board of Missions and Church Extension of the Methodist Church. This new plan seeks to meet certain difficult aspects of the problem of the town and country church. Its salient feature is the creation of a new order of lay missionaries attached to the land as permanent citizens of the community and giving much time to religious ministry. These men will be commissioned missionaries of the board but will not be subject to appointment by the annual conference authorities; they cannot be removed from the rural field.

These missionaries will live upon and operate farm acquired and held by the division in locations where op portunities for Christian service are present. They will be real "dirt farmers" with a program of church work jointly developed in accordance with the needs of the field. They will be farmer-preachers permanently residing in the community and sharing all the duties and responsibilitie of citizens.

Such missionaries will be guaranteed an annual base salary in cash, plus "home, food, and fiber," or all home and family needs as produced on the farm. The money will be derived from the cash crops produced and from the church or churches served by the missionaries.

If these sources do not produce the full salary, the dif ference will be paid by the Home Division. All cash above the salary will be used to pay for the farms, estab lish additional farm units, and make possible the other services of the missions.

In certain cases there may be two homes on the same mission farm. One of these will be occupied by an "in tern," or associate, serving under the direction of the lay missionary minister. The intern may be preparing fo service as a commissioned rural missionary, or he may be a consecrated young farmer whom the church desires to assist in securing a farm of his own. In the latter case he would also be dedicated to Christian service in the com munity in which he finally settles.

It has been found that many young men contemplating or already in training for the ministry are much interested in this new form of Christian life service. Undoubtedly there will be a similar interest among persons now in preparation for or serving as teachers of agricultural vocations.

The new missionaries will be trained men. Their preparation will include study in agriculture and theology. The minimum educational qualification will be graduation in a course which includes a major in agriculture and certain courses in religion. This plan represents a departure in Protestant missionary procedure. It will solve certain hitherto insuperable difficulties in rural work.

It will provide the continuous leadership of an able man whose training adjusts him to the tasks at hand. It will insure an adequate support. It will remove an attitude of mind that in effect depreciates or stigmatizes the country preacher. It will attach the worker to the community as an active participant in all its affairs. It will tend to bridge the psychological gap that sometimes exists between the educated preacher and the plain people of the countryside.

Don E. Schooler, paster of a church with a congregation of 2,100 in Chickasha, Oklahoma, a city of 20,000 people, has developed a Larger Parish plan of urban-rural co-operation which I commend most heartily to other large town and city churches.

This larger parish contains three pastoral charges: Epworth, "the mother church"; the Frisco Avenue–Ninnekah charge, a small mission church in Chickasha and Ninnekah; and the Chickasha Circuit composed of four country churches located near Chickasha. One of the churches on the Chickasha Circuit is a consolidated schoolhouse appointment.

The Epworth Church has supplemented mission board appropriations sufficiently to provide young, well-trained college men for all the churches of the parish. Ray Lawler, pastor of the Frisco Avenue–Ninnekah charge, gets a salary of $2,300. The churches themselves pay $1,300, the conference mission board $400, and the Epworth Church $600. Roy Rowlan, pastor of the Chickasha Circuit, receives a salary of $2,400, the churches paying $1,400, the conference mission board $400, and the Epworth Church $600. All pastors are provided with comfortable, furnished parsonages.

The pastor of the Frisco Avenue–Ninnekah charge preaches each Sunday morning and evening at Frisco Avenue and each Sunday afternoon at Ninnekah. The pastor of the Chickasha Circuit likewise preaches three times each Sunday, giving each church three services per month. He also arranges one additional service a month at each point for some visiting preacher or layman. These additional services are usually cared for by the laymen of the Epworth Church.

The pastor spends at least two full days each week visiting in the community where he is to preach the following Sunday. This pastor traveled twenty thousand miles during the work of his circuit last year.

This arrangement has continued for two years with most gratifying results. The Frisco Avenue–Ninnekah membership has increased 30 per cent, the attendance 100 per cent, and the salary and general budget more than 80 per cent. The Chickasha Circuit has had an increase of 50 in membership. In addition the attendance has doubled and the contributions have tripled. Each charge is completely autonomous in the management of its own program and affairs. While each pastor and charge carries on its own program, the pastors meet regularly for consultation and fellowship. This is regarded as one of the most valuable features of the entire program.

Some fifteen men and women in the Epworth Church have given themselves enthusiastically to this enterprise to assure its success. Each week there are published and distributed to all the laymen of the parish more than one thousand copies of the *Larger Parish News* as a means of information and inspiration.

Large town and city churches of any denomination may thus through a program of urban-rural co-operation strengthen the work of their denomination in territory adjacent to their own location.

Part-time ministers are being used by a number of denominations, especially the younger ones, to establish their churches and provide church services for many rural communities which are not able to support a full-time ministry. These part-time ministers help support themselves by clerking in stores, or teaching school, or by farming, or other types of employment during the week, giving their week ends to visiting among and preaching for small town and country churches. Some churches speak of these ministers as lay preachers. Churches often begin with this type of service and through the co-operation of interested and enthusiastic laymen in the field develop into churches capable of supporting a minister who can devote all of his time to the work of the church in the community.

Part-time ministers who have largely supported themselves by other types of employment have played a glorious part across the years in the spread of the gospel and the establishment of the church. The strength of the churches in the mission field today lies in the vigor and enthusiasm of lay or part-time preachers. If this plan works in mission fields, and it does, it can be used effectively by our churches in the homeland.

This type of ministry needs to be magnified and honored in America. Without this kind of ministry many small rural communities will have to go without the gospel. The recruiting and training of such a ministry will make it possible for many of our larger town and city churches to develop a Larger Parish plan and enrich their own spiritual life. Experience has taught us that we cannot close our country churches and transplant their memberships to our town and city churches without great numerical loss. A program of this kind will enable us to minister to small but deserving groups in their own environment and at the same time strengthen and revitalize many of our larger town and city churches.

CHAPTER VII

A Rural Church Program

SOMEONE has said, "To run a church without a schedule is like trying to run a train service without a time table."

Every church should have a well-defined program. A pastor will find it advantageous to work out such a program at the beginning of the year in conference with his leaders. He cannot work out an adequate program in one evening. Some pastors hold all-day retreats to plan their program for the year. In order that he may give intelligent leadership in such a meeting, the pastor will, of course, want to think through a program himself before calling his leaders together; but his workers will have valuable suggestions, and when worked out together it becomes the program of the church and not that of the pastor. When it has been worked out, it should be printed or duplicated and posted to be used as a guide to the various activities of the year.

There follow some special features which with some variations can be worked into any rural church program to good advantage.

Much emphasis has already been placed upon evangelism, church-school work, the every-member canvass, and women's work. It is unnecessary to describe here the methods of procedure in these fields. If they are not well known, the various church boards will furnish an abundance of material dealing with the questions involved in these particular fields of service. In former chapters we have discussed the church's responsibility for the soil, for public health, and for the recreational life of the people. We have also discussed the use of other community agencies in the building of the kingdom. I have pointed out the need for the church to include these things in its over-all program and have given some general suggestions as to how it can be done. Here are other program features which merit your careful consideration.

WORSHIP SERVICES

First of all, the place and importance of the Sunday worship services should be emphasized. Some rural pastors have too often used the public worship services to publicize and promote certain community enterprises which surely should have their support, and the church's support, but should not be carried into a regular worship service. Do not make a booster service out of your worship service.

The Sunday worship service should bring to the worshipers a consciousness of the divine presence and nearness. It ought to be a spiritual mountaintop experience for all desiring a closer fellowship and walk with God. This being true, rural worship services should be as carefully planned as city services.

The service should be conducted in an orderly and impressive fashion. It should never be crowded or rushed. The spirit of this service will be marred or helped by the attitude of the pastor toward it. Cleverness and showmanship are out of order here. If the pastor has carefully planned the service and approaches it with dignity and reverence, his people will catch his spirit, and a helpful worship service will result. If the pastor is haphazard in his pulpit behaviour, gaudy or sloven in his dress, careless or jocular in making his announcements, the worship service will be marred. Rural pastors need to learn to approach and conduct their worship services with dignity.

HYMNS

Hymns constitute such an important part of a worship service that they need to be selected with great care. A pastor should always select his own hymns. A great New York pastor says he takes two hours each week to select the hymns which he uses in his worship services on Sunday. You may not take as much time to select your hymns, but this incident emphasizes the importance of care in their selection. Hymns for a worship service should help create a worshipful atmosphere and prepare the hearts of the worshipers for the reception of your message. This cannot be done if they are selected hurriedly by a song leader or at random on a volunteer basis by members of your congregation. The selection of the hymns which you use on Sunday is one of the most important features of your preparation for a worship service.

RURAL LIFE SUNDAY

Rural Life Sunday is a day observed by church organizations throughout the nation. It occurs the fifth

Sunday after Easter. It was first observed in 1929 at the suggestion of the International Association of Agricultural Missions. The day is used for the invocation of God's blessing upon the seed, the fruits of the soil, and the cultivators of the earth—for the consideration of justice for agriculture and the spiritual values of rural life.

Both rural and city churches observe the day in many places. Parishes consisting of several churches should perhaps make it a parish day for all the churches, with dinner on the ground. It will be helpful for country and city pastors to exchange pulpits on this day. Local agricultural organizations such as Four-H clubs, the Future Farmers of America, the Farm Bureau, Grange, and Farmer's Union should be invited to attend and share in the benefits.

If the fifth Sunday after Easter is not convenient, the day may be observed at your discretion. Many denominational headquarters will furnish suggestions for the appropriate observance of the day, or you may secure such information from the Home Missions Council of North America, 297 Fourth Avenue, New York 10, New York.

DECORATION DAY

Decoration Day should be included on every rural church program. The day is more generally observed in the North than in the South. It should be observed by all sections. By observing this day we pay due respect to our sacred dead and remind ourselves of an obligation which we owe to those who have gone before us. That many rural cemeteries are allowed to grow up in weeds is a reflection upon the communities. The observance of this day will furnish incentive and opportunity for cleaning and beautifying the cemeteries. Where possible let the weeds and grass be cut and removed from the cemetery before the community gathers with its flowers for the graves. The memorial service should be carefully arranged in advance. Such a service offers a wonderful opportunity to emphasize the fact that this life does not end all; the debt we owe to the founders of our nation, the preservers of our liberty, and all who have had a part in paving the way for the life we now enjoy; our obligation to hand down to those who come after us the spiritual heritage we have received from our fathers; and the glorious gospel hope of reunion with our loved ones in the life which is to come.

A good speaker and appropriate music will add greatly to the effectiveness of the observance.

VACATION CHURCH SCHOOLS

Wide-awake rural churches are now holding vacation church schools. In small communities the churches have oftentimes found it advantageous to hold union or cooperative vacation church schools. These schools supplement the work of the regular church school which is carried on from Sunday to Sunday through the year.

Most of our children are sadly lacking in their religious training and education. "Only one child in three of public-school age is enrolled in a Sunday school of any faith. Of those enrolled only 50 per cent are in average attendance." [1] Those who attend the fifty-two church-school sessions on Sunday in a year get only twenty-six hours of instruction if they are present every Sunday. Many of those attending our church schools on Sunday receive very little religious instruction in the home. And it is reasonable to assume that those who do not attend get even less.

Protestant children are getting less religious education than any other group. The Catholic Church provides 200 hours of religious education a year for its 8,500,000 children. The Jews provide their children with 335 hours of religious training a year. Protestant children get only 26 hours of religious training and education if they attend their church school every Sunday in the year without missing a Sunday! And this training is too often of very poor quality.

In view of these facts every rural church or community should plan for a vacation church school as a supplement for the work which is done on Sunday. Such schools should be carefully planned and conducted for as many days as possible. The average vacation church school covers a period of two weeks. Where possible, more time should be used.

SUMMER CAMPS

A summer camp should be planned for the young people of your charge or parish or group ministry unit. Only a small number can attend the regular assemblies on col-

[1] Mark A. Dawber, *Rebuilding Rural America* (New York: Friendship Press, 1937), p. 111.

lege campuses and other established centers. Costs and distances make such a camping experience impossible for many who need its benefits and inspiration.

When a camp might be impossible on a cash basis, young people could likely bring from their homes canned goods and other foodstuffs adequate for the needs of such an outing.

A carefully worked out program of recreation, study, worship, and fellowship should be arranged in advance, along with rules and regulations to govern the campers. The pastor should be in charge of the camp and should have a dean of boys and a dean of girls as his assistants.

An association like this on the part of the pastor with his young people will endear him to them, overcome their reserve in his presence, and open up the way for many helpful conferences and other services.

A one-day-and-night camp is better than no camp at all.

FOURTH OF JULY

A Fourth of July service should be held in every circuit. Perhaps a Fourth of July picnic or circuit fellowship meeting could be arranged and a patriotic program rendered, including an address on "Citizenship," or "Patriotism in Time of Peace," or "America, the Beautiful" by the pastor or some guest speaker.

This service can be made more impressive by carefully selected hymns or songs. A school band or orchestra could be used to advantage. Patriotic decorations will also add to the occasion.

Harvest Festival Service

A harvest festival service should be held following the harvests, September and October being the preferable months. Many communions have abandoned such a festival, but it should be revived. Harvest time is an occasion for thanksgiving and praise. It was so observed by the children of Israel under divine command.

Surely the Christian church, and especially those churches serving in rural areas, should observe a harvest festival, not under compulsion but out of love and gratitude to God for his goodness and bounty. This harvest festival should not be substituted for or supplanted by our general Thanksgiving Day service. We need a festival in connection with agriculture in which the mystery of seed and soil and harvest may be used to remind us of our dependence upon God and of his never-failing mercy in the provision which he has made for our physical as well as spiritual well-being.

This service offers an opportunity for distinctive decorations which could hardly be appropriately used at any other time. Care should be taken that coarseness and crudity do not crowd out artistry and symmetry. In place of regular flowers, autumn leaves, decorative gourds, ears of corn, small pumpkins, sheaves, vegetables, and colorful fruits may be artistically arranged about the church entrance and around the chancel and pulpit with a most impressive effect.

Representatives of agricultural agencies should be especially invited. If lunch is served, a program could be arranged for the afternoon with several addresses on the contribution the rural areas make to American life.

PAGEANTS

Joe H. Carter's pageant "The Giant of the Wastelands" showing man's neglect of the land on which and from which he lives will make a delightful and profitable Sunday winter evening program. Young people can put this and other pageants on most effectively.

ARBOR DAY

Arbor Day was first observed in Nebraska in 1872. Thirty-eight of our states have since enacted laws for the observance of the day. In other states such a day is observed by proclamation of the governor, authorization of the superintendent of education, or by other action. In general the day is observed early in the year in the South, while it is set nearer spring in the northern states. Arbor Day has become a symbol of our faith in the future. While closely allied with economic and aesthetic ideas, the day also takes the form of a patriotic event. Arbor Day is tree-planting day. Because of the importance of the forest tree to our individual and public welfare, it is natural that in many communities the day's activities should be marked by interest in tree-planting programs. On this day we are reminded of the importance of our national and privately owned forests and the possibility of replanting much of our waste land to forest trees. As parks for public use and enjoyment have increased, villages, cities, towns, school districts, and countrysides have realized more and more the importance of trees and have used Arbor Day as a means to encourage planting them. Hospitals and churches have also become interested and sought to beautify and make more comfortable their surroundings by tree-planting programs.

This is why Arbor Day observance is included as a part of the rural church program. God loves the beautiful, and the church and parsonage grounds should be beautiful. Why not use Arbor Day to encourage the planting of trees and shrubs about the church property? It is often barren, ugly, uninviting. Why should not church grounds be the most inviting spot in the community and the parsonage home surroundings an example of how other homes in the community might appear? Bleak, barren, ugly, unkept church and parsonage grounds are as much a reflection upon the aesthetic tastes, or lack of them, of a pastor as they are of the church membership.

Why should not our churches, having beautified their own property and grounds, join hands in a co-operative effort for village and community beautification?

Your state forest service will co-operate with you in an Arbor Day observance and program of community beautification.

The special program features and days thus far suggested have been given in the order of our seasons. They therefore constitute a skeleton program for the entire year. There are, however, some other possibilities.

Fifth Sunday Week Ends

Fifth Sundays can be used to good advantage on circuits or by groups of rural churches for rural chautauquas or rural life institutes and conferences.

Many subjects may be discussed in such meetings: Financing the Country Church; The Social and Recreational Life of Rural People; The Rural Church and Community Health; A Rural Beautification Program; The Rural Church and the Church School; Woman's Work in the Rural Church. Any number of other appropriate subjects could be listed.

Such an occasion offers opportunity for fellowship, worship, inspiration, recreation, and the enlarging of one's circle of friends and acquaintances.

Night Schools

Where desired night schools could be held one night a week for a stated number of weeks for the discussion of subjects of vital interest to rural people. Here are some suggestions for subjects: Building the Farm Home; Soil Building and Care; The Dairy Cow and Her Care; Feeding and Marketing Hogs; Poultry Raising for the Average Farmer; Growing Forage Crops; The Soybean as a Feed Crop; Agricultural Products for Industry; Prevention of Disease; Sanitation.

High school and college agricultural teachers, county and home demonstration agents, doctors and trained nurses will be happy to co-operate in such an effort. The United States Department of Agriculture will gladly furnish material for use and distribution in such classes.

Other bureaus and agencies in Washington will supply
material upon any subject to be discussed.

VISUAL EDUCATION PROGRAMS

The United States Department of Agriculture, agri
cultural and mechanical college extension services, state
boards of health, and many church boards will gladly
furnish free movie films for visual education programs

WOMEN'S GROUPS

Oftentimes in small country churches a women'
group seems impossible. But if cars are available and
the distances between the churches are not too great, the
women of near-by churches of the same or different de
nominations might organize to meet at least monthly. I
the churches are too widely scattered for a regular weekly
or monthly meeting, a few interested women in each
church might organize into a circle of the group to meet
in their own community monthly or oftener. Then all of
the circles could come together for a quarterly meeting of
the group as a whole. It is better generally for the women
to have their own quarterly meeting occasion, which
might be an all-day affair with a covered dish luncheon
at the noon hour. In this way many more of the rural
women can be enlisted in the work of the women'
group and given a privilege which they certainly deserve

YOUNG PEOPLE'S GROUPS

A similar situation often exists in small country
churches with reference to young people. A small rural
church may not have enough young people to form an

effective and enthusiastic young people's organization. In such a situation the young people of the several small churches might be organized into a group or union organization meeting weekly or monthly on Sunday afternoon in one of the churches, perhaps in rotation, or on a week night at some designated center.

MEN'S CLUBS

Luncheon clubs meeting weekly are popular in our urban centers. They afford opportunities for fellowship and fun and the discussion of many subjects of urban and national interest. Some rural pastors in small towns and on circuits where their men do not have any such civic organizations are organizing men's luncheon clubs meeting at least monthly. Any subject of interest to the church or community may be discussed at these meetings. The clubs should always be conducted in a rather informal manner. Many disinterested men and nonmembers have become interested in the work of such clubs and as a result later have found their places in the membership and other activities of the church.

CHURCH PUBLICITY PROGRAMS

If small town and country churches are to get the publicity to which they are entitled, their pastors will have to prepare their own publicity material. Editors of country papers are almost without exception glad to carry free of charge the announcements of any rural church in their area. Furnish your editor with a schedule of your regular services and ask him to carry it from week to week. He will be glad to do so. Then furnish him with a carefully written news story, preferably a typewritten copy, of your various gatherings and meetings. When you are having a special service which deserves more than the regular publicity, write it up in news story form for your editor. But learn how to write news stories. Editors want it done a certain way. Once you know how to write your notices and stories, your publicity problem is solved in so far as the newspaper is concerned. If you simply report your meetings over the telephone or give the editor a few scribbled notes, leaving him or one of his helpers to write the story, you will likely be disappointed in the result. If the editor is giving your church space in his paper for its publicity, you ought to be glad to prepare well-written copy on the event you want publicized. Write your own stories and write them well, and both you and the editor will be pleased.

Also every church should own a printing or duplicating machine. One can now be purchased for a very reasonable sum. Church bulletins, programs, and financial statements are then possible. With such a machine the pastor can get out a monthly bulletin of considerable size for his church or circuit. A machine for duplicating post cards is now available for only a few dollars. It can be used to send out special announcements, to announce in advance your appearance at a given church and your sermon subjects, and to follow up absentees from church and church-school services.

The Lord's cause deserves to be publicized. Therefore publicize your church!

The Rural Minister and His Training

I HAVE sought through questionnaires sent to district superintendents, rural pastors, and laymen to ascertain, if possible, what constitutes an ideal rural pastor. The results have been disappointing and unsatisfying.

The best description of an ideal rural pastor was written by a district superintendent who has had years of experience in dealing with rural ministers and churches:

1. He should love rural people because they are people and believe they are entitled to the best ministry within his power to render anywhere.
2. He should love the open spaces and the out-of-doors and be so acquainted with the interests and customs of rural people as to feel at home among them and to make them feel at ease in his presence.
3. He should be able to interpret and apply religion in terms of the needs for the whole life of the people he serves.
4. He should have a wife who sees eye to eye with him in these matters and lends her fullest co-operation.
5. He should study his problems as diligently as any city pastor studies his and seek solutions of them for his people's sake, just as he might elsewhere for his reputation's sake.

The laymen had difficulty in writing down their ideas about an ideal rural pastor. Most of their replies indicate that their general conception of an ideal pastor is a good man, a good preacher, a good visitor. But a few excerpts from their numerous replies to the questionnaire may help to give a composite picture of an ideal rural pastor.

"A genuine Christian gentleman with a zeal for saving souls and a zeal for work, with education enough for him to feel at ease among all classes of people," wrote one.

Three fourths of the laymen who replied to the questionnaire wanted their pastors to be community leaders, though some of them wanted to limit them to church, school, and social affairs.

One good woman wanted her pastor to be a community leader but did not want him to become "a sort of chamber-of-commerce pastor."

"A good mixer, one who will visit his people and others who need his help and guidance." "One who will visit his people" was put down perhaps oftener than anything else.

"A pastor who is honest, not only the kind of honesty that keeps a man's fingers out of his neighbor's till, but that finer honesty that will not allow a man to give less than his best, the kind of honesty that makes him count not his hours but his duties and opportunities for rendering service."

"Not lazy," a number of laymen wrote. No preacher, whether in the country or the city, will ever attain large success if he is afraid to work.

But very few of any group replying to the questionnaire seemed to feel or to recognize that the pastor has any responsibility to his people or to the community, other than the "spiritual welfare" of those among whom he serves. I want, therefore, to give the testimony of some others on this subject.

Douglas Ensminger, who is in charge of Rural Sociology extension work under the United States Department of Agriculture, in an article entitled "If I Were a Rural Pastor" had this to say:

I would want to know and understand the basic social and economic trends of rural life.

I would want to know and understand the community of which the church is a part.

I would want to know what the basic problems or needs of the community are—man-land relationships, adjustment in farming economy, marketing, health, religion, school, and so forth.

I would want to know what agencies and organizations there are in the county working with rural people, and what they are doing or might do to help solve problems in the community.[1]

Mrs. Calvin Perdue, who described herself as "a rural homemaker, a mother, and an interested church member," said:

We have a right to expect the church to minister to the spiritual and social needs of the family, to correlate all agencies for community betterment, and to promote and stimulate American democracy. The social and economic needs of a rural community must of necessity differ from urban centers. "The kind of church I would like to have in

[1] *Christian Rural Fellowship Bulletin*, November, 1945.

my community" would desire a minister who is interested not only in soul salvation but soil salvation, the saving and conserving of all human and material resources.

Charles J. Galpin, a layman who for many years has been a leader in the Country Life Movement of the United States, certainly deserves to be heard.

If I were a rural minister, I would try to gear all my efforts in with the great general aim of the leaders of rural America to build a worthy rural civilization. My aim would be a parish and a church of distinction that would in no sense be out of place in the coming civilization of rural America.[2]

To meet the broadened conception of the rural minister's obligation as suggested by Ensminger, Galpin, Mrs. Perdue, and others, and for them to become "ideal rural pastors," special training and preparation will certainly be necessary.

Many of our leaders contend that it is not "the kind of training but the kind of men who are trained" that will count the most in the solution of our rural problem. It is true that "there is more in the man than there is in the land," but a great many are firm in the conviction that we need a broader type of training for our rural ministry, or should I just say our ministry. Since a very large percentage of our churches are rural churches, and a very large percentage of our young men trained for the ministry must begin their ministry in rural churches—and only a few of them can, or will, ever serve city churches—should we not have a more general training for rural fields. If no differentiation is to be made in

[2] *Ibid.*, October, 1940.

the training of our ministers, would it not be the part of wisdom to provide training for the much larger percentage which will always serve in rural areas? And if, as dependable surveys indicate, nearly three fourths of those serving on city church boards come from the country, will not men trained for a rural ministry, with some special study of city problems, be widely acceptable to city congregations? Should someone say most of our preachers come from rural areas and already have the rural viewpoint without special training, is it not safe to reply that even country pastors will find it advantageous to have some careful training in rural economics, rural sociology, and the problems faced daily by our rural constituency? A growing number are convinced that such a training is necessary for our ministry.

In this connection the conclusions of Martin Schroeder, Rural Work Representative of the Board of Missions of the United Lutheran Church in America, are important.

The assumption still exists that one type of preacher leaving school could serve either city or country church with equal ease and efficiency. From my own student days I well remember a lecturer who, belonging himself to the old "no difference" school, addressed us hopefuls: "Gentlemen, it may do you no harm to spend the first five or ten years of your ministry in a country church." The man who lectured might have been heard in almost any seminary.

The writer fell for it. Promptly upon graduation he assumed the pastorate of a tiny, isolated parish. Five years passed. Ten years passed. He was still in the country. About that time he wrote an article on "The Attractions of the

101

Rural Pastorate." In that article he went the lecturer one better. Instead of speaking of five to ten years among the farmers, the advice was given to set aside at least the first ten to fifteen years in the rural community. Since then ten more cycles of summer and winter have joined their predecessors, and still he finds himself, though in a changed relation, attracted to the country church.

Today after more than two decades of intimate contact with rural church life, he sees again the necessity of revising his estimate of the length of time a ministerial candidate should plan to spend in the country. To a man casting about for a field of labor he would say, if at all there is any serious thought in the direction of the small community congregation, to set aside the first forty years of his ministry for the purpose and for the time being eliminate notions of the enchanting city pulpit from his mind altogether. From the beginning it must be one thing or the other. Mixing the two separate types of labor in mind and practice is hard on preacher and congregations. In other words, a continuously settled ministry is prerequisite to achieve fortification of the rural church.

The wholesale closing of country churches must be ascribed to a great extent to preachers who were victims of the popular fancy that the city is the only place of the up-and-coming man of God to find a responsive field. Denominational guidance, with few shining exceptions, has failed uniformly in either maintaining or rehabilitating the resident rural pastor. Witness the tens of thousands of liquidated rural churches, a waste in which religious leaders are not guiltless, though a belated change in attitude becomes more and more evident.

To assume that preparation for the rural ministry does not require special training is a too-common fallacy. With this same sort of reasoning one might consider that a teacher or physician may work his way through any course leading to a general degree, hoping that the question of skill in a special line will take care of itself in due time. Our city-located theological schools train future pastors with the more or less alluring near-by city churches as ever-present seducers to fill head and heart with city ideologies. Of all such institutions of every denomination and description only twenty-seven in the entire country give any semblance of recognition that a great portion of their students will have to work in sparsely settled districts. The result is many an unhappy ministry, the man finding himself in places for which God never intended him.[3]

The movement in behalf of specialized training for rural ministers is rapidly gaining ground. The Southern Rural Life Conference report of 1943 indicated that the movement is beginning to reach back into pre-theological courses.

A number of state colleges are co-operating in this matter. For illustration, a working agreement for the benefit of ministerial students has been achieved between Iowa State College and the Theological Seminary of the University of Dubuque. The courses are divided into two sections. The first section consists of six weeks on the campus of the State College of Agriculture.

Section one:—Six professors serving on the staff of the Iowa State College are sent to the University of Dubuque as an extension service of the college. Each of these professors is responsible for one section of instruction which lasts for two hours a day for one week. The six weeks run consecutively. Theological students

[3] Quoted with permission from *Christian Rural Fellowship Bulletin* No. 88 by Dr. Martin Schroeder.

receive credit for these courses under the subject titles of "Rural Sociology" and "Rural Church Technique I." These courses are on a graduate level.

The costs of the courses are the same as those of any seminary courses. No tuition is charged. Board and room must be provided by the participant, with the exception of the regularly enrolled theological student. The salaries of the visiting professors are paid by the state college through extension service. However, their traveling expenses between Ames and Dubuque and their meals and lodging while on the campus are provided by the University of Dubuque.

This type of co-operative enterprise is cleared with the state board of education, and the entire session is handled as a service of the extension department.

Section two:—The courses offered on the campus of the Iowa State College are entitled "The Farm Survey School" and "Rural Pastors." Three areas in agriculture are explored: agronomy, animal husbandry, farm management.

These courses are so arranged that they may be used as supporting credit at the state college for those desiring to work for their master's degrees in rural sociology or as regular credit in rural sociology at the University of Dubuque. Students enrolling pay the regular six weeks' tuition charge which amounts to twenty-five dollars. They also provide their own board and room.

These courses are taught by the resident staff of the Iowa State College. Credits are transferred from the registrar's office there to the Theological Seminary.

Rural pastors' schools, brief college sessions, institutes, coaching conferences, brief internships, work camps, and travel seminars are being used to train our pastors better for their rural fields. More such schools are being held across the nation this year than ever before in our history.

In this connection the importance of longer-term rural pastorates should be emphasized. Mary Heald Williamson in an interesting article in the *Methodist Rural Fellowship Bulletin* for June, 1942, quotes a friend as saying:

When a man wants to move before he has served a five year pastorate, both he and his church face a sort of judgment day. We don't have a foreign missionary spending a couple of years learning the language of a country and then move him on to another country for a similar experience. It takes more than two years to learn the language of an American community.

She then points out that we have too many migrant ministers, ministers who never remain in a pastorate for over one or two years.

A small college president, refusing the presidency of a great state university, explained his refusal by declaring: "I have taken the clock apart to see what makes it go. Now I want to stay until it is running in good order."

Are we not in a constant state of taking the church to pieces to see what makes the wheels go round and then deserting to a new field of work? In New York rural Methodist preachers are now changing fields at the rate of every 2.9 years. No wonder that various pieces of church machinery are strewed about the community in bad repair.

105

Difficult situations cannot be solved by moving out of them. They cannot be solved that way on the mission field, neither can they be solved that way on the home field. We need to learn to face our problems and to stay with a given task until it is completed. Our laymen cannot move out of these impossible situations. We must find a cure for the mobility which afflicts so many of our ministers.

Short-term pastorates are unquestionably the bane of our small town and country churches. If a minister would spend at least seven years in a community, one long-term pastor suggests, he could help train a generation of young people thirteen to twenty years of age. During this formative period of their lives he could exercise a wonderful influence for good which would bear fruit across many years to come.

We must find a cure for the mobility which afflicts so many ministers. Longer pastorates are necessary if we are to rehabilitate our rural churches, if these churches and pastors are to become the influence in the community they ought to be.

Why do our pastors move so often? Many move because, as it has been suggested, it is easier to move out of an apparently impossible situation than to solve it. Roy L. Smith once said, "Many pastors move because their churches won't." Evidences of this are available.

Many move because of their lack of training, their lack of sufficient resourcefulness to remain for an indefinite period of years. Many move because their churches ask for a change, and the churches ask for a change because their pastors do not meet the pulpit requirements of the church and community or are lacking in community leadership ability. Too often this is because of inadequate training.

But the majority move with the hope of improving their economic conditions. Many young men go into the ministry expecting to devote their lives to rural work, but when they find it impossible to meet the increasing demands of growing families upon the salaries they are getting, they accept churches which are able to give them more adequate support.

This question of ministerial support will be discussed in the next chapter.

CHAPTER IX

Rural Church Problems

Adequate Ministerial Support

ADEQUATE ministerial support is perhaps the biggest problem before the rural church at the present time.

Edwin E. Sundt suggests that with too many the ministry has become

a career and a profession with an ever-lessening sense of duty, religious urgency, and devotion to humanitarian attainments. Bishoprics and lucrative pulpits supply the motive for service, and few have any difficulty discerning "the leading of the Holy Spirit or a divine call" when such an opportunity includes added social prestige, material security, and comforts. This must change if town and country churches are to prosper in this day and generation. Somehow the service motive must be recaptured by Christian ministers. The spirit of heroic self-sacrifice, as truly romantic and urgent in the homeland as the call to any foreign mission field, must become once more part and parcel of every rural worker's heart and soul.[1]

Mr. Sundt realizes, as we all do, that the "labourer is worthy of his hire" and that something must be done to provide more adequate support for the rural minister. He suggests larger parishes as a possible solution to this problem.

[1] Edwin E. Sundt, *The Country Church and Our Generation* (copyright 1932 by Fleming H. Revell Company), p. 140.

We have now come to realize that it requires a population of one thousand people to support a single successfully financed Protestant church. Once this is applied in practice, the salary question will care for itself. On the other hand, as long as we insist upon maintaining eight, ten, or more churches in areas of one thousand people, or less, we will have to accept the inevitable results. A thousand people cannot support ten religious organizations. Such religious taxation is neither Christian nor warranted.[2]

Church leaders in a midwestern area said in a recent conference report:

Maps of our districts show that we have built too many churches and built them too close together. Horse and buggy distances do not fit into automobile days.

Our Year Book reports too many church schools with an average attendance of between ten and twenty. Often a few removals leave a church almost without members. Such churches, if kept open, have little leadership, weak programs, and little appeal to outsiders. They are very likely to develop rebellion against our system and . . . methods. . . .

The solution, if solution there be, will not be for the ministers and the church to do more things for the people, but to teach and persuade the people to do more things for themselves and for their neighbors. One of the things they must be persuaded to do is to drive farther to fewer but larger and more efficient churches. They are doing this for schools, for trading, and for politics. It will be necessary also for religion. We need a long-time program looking to fewer churches and better ones reaching out to greater distances. The present and prospective shortage of ministers makes this all the more necessary.[3]

[2] *Ibid.*
[3] *Methodist Rural Fellowship Bulletin*, November, 1943.

This is not an argument for retrenchment but for better and stronger churches and a more effective and better supported ministry. Small "pockets" of people will have to be served, must be served, by this larger church in small chapels or the homes of the people where a few neighbors can be brought together. We have consolidated schools; we are now in many instances going to have to think in terms of more consolidated churches.

Marcius E. Taber has some pertinent things to say:

The salary estimate is made as a lump sum. Lump sum payments mean that the more a minister spends for car maintenance, books, and attendance on training institutes, the less he has for himself and vice versa. For all practical purposes he is being paid NOT to call; for the more calls he makes, the less salary he has to spend on himself.[4]

It has been suggested that the parish should own a car and maintain it for the use of the minister, and thus leave the family car for his wife to use while doing her church work. Taber proposes a plan less drastic than that. The United States Post Office Department now pays rural carriers six cents a mile for the distance traveled while carrying the mail. Many business concerns which have representatives on the open road driving their own cars pay so much per mile traveled in the interest of the employer. The church might adopt a similar policy. Such a policy certainly has much in its favor.

[4] "Methodism's Horse and Buggy Salary System," *Methodist Rural Fellowship Bulletin*, Summer, 1945.

Consolidated churches or larger parishes, on the other hand, will make it possible for mission boards to provide more adequate salaries.

The every-member canvass will provide an adequate salary in many situations where haphazard, hit-and-miss methods still prevail. The wise pastor will see that an every-member canvass is conducted in each of the churches he serves at the beginning of the church year. This canvass should be conducted perhaps a month before the beginning of the new church year, so that the official board and the pastor will know how to make their plans for the ensuing year. Every member of the church, old and young, should be asked for a pledge. Sermons on stewardship and the distribution of stewardship and tithing literature, which is easily obtainable, will prepare the way for increased giving on the part of the church.

Many rural churches have budgets which include the pastor's salary, apportionments on benevolences, church-school supplies, insurance, lights, heating, and such incidentals as may be foreseen. Pledges are taken to cover the budget, foreseen obligations of the church, and are paid weekly through envelopes in the church school. The financial secretary and treasurer should keep a record of all contributions in a permanent record book especially prepared for this purpose, which can be secured from any publishing house at nominal cost. The pastor's salary and all other obligations should be paid monthly.

One board of missions is locating farmer-pastors on farms purchased by the board in numerous strategic

111

centers. Many other church-farms are being used advantageously in many sections of the country.

Other denominations in many places are purchasing farms for the use of their pastors. They are thus enabled to have some cows, chickens, hogs, an orchard, a garden, and a pasture. They can also raise some cash crops with which to supplement the support that the churches are able to give them. Such provision often makes it possible for a community to have a resident pastor when otherwise it could not. It helps to stabilize the rural minister on the land.

Oftentimes these farms are gifts. Ralph A. Felton of Drew Theological Seminary says that six out of ten such farms are bequests. Twenty-three per cent of them come from living donors. His survey of this field indicates that only 17 per cent of them have been purchased by the church.

Churches providing or inheriting such farms should secure pastors who have had some training in an agricultural college, so that the pastor may become a leader in developing agriculture along the latest scientific lines and thus help to raise the living standards of the community.

The Town and Country Church in March, 1945, carried an interesting article by Russel Hoy on "A Small Farm for the Pastor." Pastor Hoy for years had served industrial and small city communities. Six and one-half years before writing the article he accepted the pastorate of a little village of about forty houses in Ohio. This village church had a membership of 120, of whom he classed 95 as active. They had difficulty in raising a budget of $850, of which $550 was paid on the pastor's salary. Church-school attendance was around 55, and there were even fewer at the worship service. Hoy, feeling a call to strictly rural work, left a county seat church of 400 members in 1938 to accept this rural village church and rented a fruit farm a few miles from the village. With "little money and lots of faith" the church was completely remodeled during his first year. This gave them necessary accommodation for a church and community program. The remodeling was paid for in three years.

But at the end of three years he decided that his rented fruit farm was too large. The official board then rented in the village a small house and lot with a barn and three acres of pasture adjoining. He moved to this place in the fall of 1941, taking with him one cow, fifty chickens, and several hogs. He sold a little excess milk to the neighbors who came to the door for it. The demand for milk increased, and he bought another cow and the next summer a third cow. From these three cows for the next three years he netted forty dollars a month for milk after buying most of the feed. He raised a couple of hogs for butchering and about four hundred chickens which he sold for broilers each year, keeping around fifty laying hens through the winter. He worked out by day among his neighbors to earn enough hay and corn for his stock.

Church membership, interest, and attendance grew. The budget and the pastor's salary increased each year.

The people were pleased to have a resident pastor living among them, the first they had ever had.

In 1944 he asked his church board to buy a parsonage farm somewhere in the community. They were reluctant to go in debt for such a purpose though they liked the idea. They then suggested that he buy such a farm himself, and one of the men agreed to loan the money on easy terms. Eight and one-half acres of pasture land were purchased one mile from the church. Sixteen adjoining acres were rented. The place was improved during the summer; and a lovely cottage home, completely modern, a barn, and a tile poultry house that would accommodate two hundred laying hens were built. After several years in his own little home he says that he is more convinced than ever that a small farm for a rural minister, a home of his own, is a most desirable thing. It makes for a longer pastorate, it helps the community accept the pastor and his family as "their own," it gives him a sense of economic security and physical exercise that is both recreational and profitable.

And what have been the results of this pastor's dedication of himself to this rural pastorate? The church budget is around $2,400, half of which is paid on the pastor's salary. The membership has grown to 221, and attendance upon the services has more than doubled. New families moving into the community, regardless of previous denominational affiliation, have joined this church. Twelve denominations are now represented in its membership.

In conclusion Hoy says:

We try to make our whole life a form of ministry. Our personal lives, our home, our neighborliness, our farm work, our preaching, our social calls, our recreation, all are a part of our ministry. We cannot divide our time and say, "Now we are doing church work." Our total work in the church and out is our ministry.

The Woodlawn charge in the Lawton, Oklahoma District under the leadership of Ernest C. Hicks, the district superintendent, in April, 1945, purchased a 160-acre farm, paid for it, and enclosed it with a new four-wire fence strung on cedar posts. Located on it was a nice, modern five-room house with electricity, butane gas, hot and cold running water, hardwood floors, and plenty of built-ins in the kitchen.

"The pastor will not farm it," the district superintendent said. "Most of the land which has been cultivated will be turned back to grass to be used for pasture. This farm will produce $560 worth of calves annually. The pastor must not farm; he must use the land to grow calves."

The churches pay $800 on the salary, the mission board $200, making a total of $1,000. This plus $560 worth of calves gives the pastor an annual income of $1,560. In addition to this he will have his garden, chickens, cow, pigs, and an orchard.

This superintendent thinks it will take too much time away from study and pastoral work to operate a farm. Calves grow while the pastor is engaged in the necessary work of the parish.

115

ATTRACTIVE CHURCH BUILDINGS

An inadequate church building is often held up as one of the problems of the rural church. There was a time when a one-room church seemed to meet the demands of the day. But a more adequate building is necessary for an expanding church program. A social and recreational room and kitchen with a few classrooms, especially for the children's division, would greatly help the small rural church in serving effectively the community. This is particularly true where school districts have been consolidated and the little church has become more than formerly the community center. Where the funds necessary for such improvement cannot be provided otherwise, they may be made possible by the adoption of the Lord's Acre plan. But many churches are still using small one-room church buildings to good advantage.

What I want to emphasize in this connection, however, is the importance of putting and keeping your little church in good repair. "Too many of our rural church buildings are the weather vanes of lack of spirituality, vitality, and vision." [5] With volunteer labor and a little money to buy lumber or paint, you can make your rural church attractive and worshipful.

The grounds of a country church should be sodded and landscaped. Nurseries will often donate shrubs and trees for such a purpose, or individuals may provide them. In many situations native shrubs and trees can be used.

[5] *Christian Rural Fellowship Bulletin*, July, 1944.

Those who have had experience in transplanting trees and shrubs will doubtless volunteer their labor to set them out.

If you are proud of your church, some professional painter will likely be glad to paint a sign with the name of your church and the days and hours of services on it as his contribution to an improvement program. Every church, even the rural one, should carry its name in some conspicuous place, so that passers-by may recognize it.

Even those who cannot afford anything more than a small one-room church should make that room attractive and worshipful on the inside. Soft and beautiful shades of paint should be used if the interior is painted. Before painting the inside of your church, visit some of the larger town and city churches and study their interior colors and decorations. They have been done by experts.

Your pulpit, chancel, and communion table can be made from pattern by some local cabinetmaker who will likely contribute his work if you will furnish the material.

An inexpensive cross can be made by a cabinetmaker for a fraction of what one will cost if bought from a church supply house. A beautiful cross on your communion table will add much to the worshipful atmosphere of your sanctuary.

Even a rural church may have a hymn board which could also be made locally. But put no other announcement boards, report boards, or posters in the area back of your pulpit which your congregation will face during a worship service. Such boards or posters are distracting.

If there is space behind the pulpit and you have no art-glass window, there are many inexpensive pictures portraying religious scenes which may be used. Perhaps someone will donate such a picture beautifully framed. However, only copies or prints of the masterpieces should be used.

A picture for such a conspicuous place or for use anywhere else in the church should be selected with great care and upon the advice of someone who has knowledge of art. I would caution against using in a prominent place any picture drawn or painted by some member of the congregation or the community, which you accept rather than risk offending some member or family belonging to the church. Though it may be an exceptionally good piece of work for an amateur, it will likely become embarrassing. Use only the work of the masters for such a purpose.

Some individual or class may furnish flowers for the altar, especially on preaching Sundays.

By using the material and talent which you have at hand you may have "a place of meeting" to which the community will be glad to come. In this way you may displace the dreariness of many a worship place, overcome a spirit of defeatism, create in the community as a whole a love for the beautiful and aesthetic, and prepare the way for other church improvements.

Church Support

The Lord's Acre plan was begun as a movement among country churches in western North Carolina in 1930. In

118

1944 approximately three thousand churches in the United States and mission fields used this plan.

The plan is that each member of a country church, and all who receive the benefits of the church, shall set aside and dedicate to the Lord some worthy portion of a farm crop or of the farm stock, raise the produce or stock, sell it, and give the cash proceeds to the church. It is the only way that many can give. For those who are already making substantial gifts, this plan is intended to be supplementary. The standard for the Lord's Acre or the Lord's Acre proceeds together with the cash gift is the tithe.

The plan has scriptural foundation. The practice of dedicating the first fruits of the land and the firstlings of the herds and flocks largely supported the services of worship and provided spiritual training in Bible days. (Deut. 12:6.)

Churches have been built or remodeled, church debts paid, church-school facilities enlarged, heating plants installed, and parsonages improved by churches of many denominations which have adopted this plan.

It is not the purpose of this plan to supplant the every-member canvass or the support of the church by cash contributions. It is suggested that it be used for property improvement purposes rather than for the salaries and the regular benevolences, though in some instances it has been used for these purposes also.

The universal testimony of those who have used the plan is that it has stimulated and increased contributions

119

to the regular budget, that few indeed have used it as an excuse for smaller cash contributions.

The Lord's Acre plan is an ideal method of stewardship training. H. C. Weber, formerly the president of the Stewardship Council of the United States and Canada, writes:

The Lord's Acre plan personalizes giving pre-eminently. Toil goes into it; sharing with the Lord that which is a daily care and concern goes into it. Forethought and watchfulness are required. The self, muscle, thought, and skill are involved. When the Lord finally gets the result, he has in his hands a significant offering.

Such a plan calls for careful advance preparation, and it is urged that any who contemplate its use write Rev. Dumont Clarke, Director Religious Department, Farmers Federation, Asheville, N. C., for suggestions and literature. Ralph A. Felton of Drew Theological Seminary has published a booklet on *The Lord's Acre* which is most interesting and informing.

LAY LEADERSHIP

Lay leadership, or the lack of it, is always raised as one of our rural problems. It is a problem, but I believe an incidental one. Everywhere you go you hear rural pastors say, "We need church-school superintendents, church-school teachers, official boards with vision, youth leaders, scout leaders." How are we going to get them? Import them? Most town and city pastors are having difficulty also in finding sufficient capable leaders for the effective organization of their churches. Furthermore, rural folk often resent imported leadership.

Untrained pastors have to blunder along as best they can with unskilled workmen. This has been happening in rural work for years. Rural churches have been served, for the most part, by unskilled and inexperienced ministers who themselves were serving, as it were, an internship in the ministry. These have been student pastors or young men just out of college. Sometimes they have been men who because of lack of training have not been able to secure more lucrative pastorates.

We cannot expect an unskilled, untrained minister to train a skilled lay leadership. But give us in the rural areas a trained ministry with a warm heart, a lot of patience, and love for folk, leave it there long enough, and lay leadership will arise from within the ranks of any given community. The Master had no trained leaders with which to begin his work, but he took twelve laymen and trained them. He could have called trained men, but he preferred to train his own leaders.

The missionary in China or Africa or India lacks "lay leadership." He has to create and train his own leaders.

If we are going to have better rural lay leadership, we are going to have to take the folk we have and train them. Where are you going to get your leaders? Right where you are. There is an undeniable advantage in training your own leadership. It will have the kind of training you want it to have. But in the ministry you have to stay long enough to do the job.

Too many ministers furnish all the leadership of a

church or charge. They succeed in a big way. But when they move on, much of their good work is dissipated because their successors do not possess the leadership they had and they have left no trained lay leadership to carry on the work. A wise pastor, interested in the continuation of his work, will train lay leaders capable of carrying on when he has been moved to another charge.

But someone asks, "How can a pastor train his leaders?" He may conduct leadership classes using the many courses that are provided by the church for that purpose. He can place in the hands of those whom he has selected as leaders books and folders on how to do the things he wants them to do. Much literature is available without cost from various boards which can be used in such a training program. In evangelistic work it has been shown that a pastor can train his workers for this necessary task, which the laymen ought to do as well as the minister, by taking with him one layman at a time as he goes out to interview people about their souls. Having learned his pastor's technique and having gained some practical experience himself, that one can in turn train other laymen the same way. Similarly a layman can be taught how to visit the sick or how to visit in the interest of the church school. If the pastor wants to train the men how to present the budget of the church to those assigned him, he can take a new solicitor with him and solicit a few subscriptions himself. But the minister must know the technique of these things himself before he can teach others how to do them.

For years now in many churches leadership training

schools have been conducted with fine results. But little special attention has been given to courses on rural work. For this reason suitable and practical courses on rural work should be immediately made available, and such courses should be offered in every leadership training school held in rural areas. These courses will be exceedingly helpful in training a competent lay leadership.

By the use of these methods, the leadership training schools, and regular church-school publications, a competent, efficient lay leadership can soon be developed for the rural church.

CHAPTER X

Successful Rural Pastorates

CHARLES KINGSLEY

CHARLES KINGSLEY has been known to more people as a poet, scientist, man of letters, university lecturer, and social reformer than as a parson. But as a graduate of two leading colleges he came in 1842 to the rural Parish of Eversley in Hampshire, England. He was then twenty-three years old and likely had little thought that he would minister to this people for a generation. But this was the only parish he ever served.

Though the son of a clergyman, he had been troubled with doubts during his youth. When he was twenty-two, God laid his hand upon him. Writing about his call to the ministry he said:

My birth night. I have been for the last hour on the sea-shore, not dreaming but thinking deeply and strongly and forming determinations which are to affect my destiny through time and eternity. Before the sleeping earth and the sleeping sea and stars, I have devoted myself to God, a vow never (if He gives me the faith I pray for) to be re-called.[1]

His parish was made up of three small hamlets with a scattered population. He described it as "peculiar for

[1] Ezra Tipple, *Some Famous Country Parishes* (New York: Abingdon Press, 1911), p. 206.

nothing but want of houses and peat bogs" and his parishioners as "remarkable only for aversion to education and a predilection to fat bacon."

When he accepted this parish, there was not a man or woman in the parish among the laboring class who could read or write. They had no school house and they had no religious instruction. The church was almost empty; the churchyard was used as a pasture for sheep; they took their offerings in a wooden saucer; a cracked basin served as a baptismal font; the altar was covered with a moth-eaten cloth, and by it stood a broken chair. And there was so much opposition to any change that when he proposed a monthly communion service, his wardens were so niggardly that he himself had to furnish the sacramental elements for the additional services. Poverty, ignorance, and superstition prevailed on every hand. Farm laborers received from 8 to 10 shillings a week for their work; and his own salary, out of which he had to contribute much to the needy of his parish, was only 150 pounds a year. It would not be an easy or remunerative pastorate. *"But he was not dismayed. Eversley needed him."* And he accepted it as a field of service for his Lord.

He became almost at once a daring, militant parson, hating sham and affectation, a kind of spiritual frontiersman. With him there was no mouthing of words or apologies. When he was only twenty-nine, he wrote:

I will not be a liar. . . . I will speak in season and out of season. . . . I will not take council with flesh and blood and flatter myself into the dream that, while every man on earth back to Abel, whoever tried to testify against the

125

world, has been laughed at, misunderstood, slandered, and that bitterest of all, by the very people he loved best, I alone am to escape. My path is clear and I will follow it.[2]

He preached retribution and warned the wicked and the oppressor of his fate. He was not given to conventional and unmeaningful phraseology. He spoke as a man alive to living men. He spoke with a passion about what was going on in the hearts and lives of his people—their sins, their sorrows, their doubts, their struggles. He discussed both local matters and national issues. And yet all who knew him and heard him were impressed with his compassion and love and the tender regard which he had for all. He seemed to love everybody and everything. But this love inspired him to speak out boldly against evil wherever he found it:

I will never believe that a man has a real love for the beautiful except he attacks the evil and the disgusting the moment he sees it. It is very easy for us to turn our eyes away from the ugly sights and so consider ourselves refined. The refined man to me is the one who cannot rest in peace with a coal mine, or a factory, or a Dorsetshire peasant's house near him in the state in which they are.[3]

He was not "lost in the country." Before many years a path was beaten to his door by men and women of note. Maurice, Dean Stanley, Harriet Beecher Stowe, Alfred Tennyson, Queen Emma of the Sandwich Islands, Thomas Hughes, Matthew Arnold, and a multitude of others came to visit in his humble country rectory. Let-

[2] Mrs. Charles Kingsley, *Charles Kingsley, His Letters and Memories of His Life* (New York: Abingdon Press, 1879), p. 69.

[3] Tipple, *op. cit.*, p. 222.

ters came to him from Africa, India, China, America, from all over the world, some of them merely addressed, "Charles Kingsley, England." Charles Kingsley glorified a country parish and made it a world center. He was honored by all, the small and the great alike.

"But he was above all things and before all things," as another has put it, "a parish clergyman," and a country parish clergyman at that.

But his influence as a country parish clergyman was due, we are told, more to *"his house to house visiting during the week"* than to his ardent, intense preaching. In his pastoral work he aimed to be all things to all men.

He could fling a flail with the thrashers in the barn, turn his swathe with the mowers in the meadow, pitch hay with the haymakers in the pasture. He knew every fox hole in the moor, the reedy hover of the pike, the still hole where the chub lay; and always had a kind word for the huntsman or the old poacher; with the farmer he could discuss the rotation of crops, with the laborer his hedging and ditching. He was at perfect ease when talking with a woman at the washtub and so was she. Children loved him and ran after him, tugging unafraid at his coat. *Daily he visited from house to house.* What a beautiful picture, this of England's most popular preacher in his generation, the cultured, scholarly, bookloving Kingsley, going from door to door in a rural community just for the sheer love of it.[4]

Notwithstanding his culture, his scholarship, his refinement, he never manifested outwardly any feeling of superiority over his poorest and most untutored parishoners. He possessed these qualities for the benefit of

[4] Kingsley, *op. cit.*, p. 30.

those less fortunate than himself. He loved the poor, the common people, whom we are told heard Jesus so gladly. One wrote: "He had a delicate, deep respect for the poor, for the good which he saw in them, for the still greater good which he hoped to see, and strove that he might see, in them."

He was always the workingman's friend, the poor man's champion. He was concerned about not only their spiritual welfare but their social and economic welfare as well. He organized clubs for the poor—a shoe club, a coal club, a maternal society; he established a loan fund and a lending library. An adult evening school was held at the rectory during the winter months. Weekly cottage lectures were given in outlying districts for the old and feeble. He championed a program of sanitation, believing that he was under obligation to the bodies of men as well as their souls and that "the state of the soul too often depends on that of the body." He declared the deliverance of men's bodies from disease and dirt and their inevitable consequences as more important than any political reform.

He was carried to his grave by villagers who had known and loved and trusted him for years. Roman Catholics and Protestants, churchmen and dissenters, Americans and English, working men and gypsies, met at his grave. Every profession, every rank, every school of thought was represented there. Soldiers and sailors were there, among them three Victoria Cross officers, men who had loved and honored him. The Master of the Foxhounds, with the huntsman and the whip, was also there. And from his beloved Chester came the dean and a deputation from the Natural Science Society which he founded. A naval officer who was present said, "I have been at many state funerals but never did I see such a sight as Charles Kingsley's."

John Frederick Oberlin

The story of Charles Kingsley as a country parson is a story that thrills the soul. But John Frederick Oberlin, who lived almost one hundred years before Kingsley, is perhaps the most publicized rural pastor of all time. He served a small mountainous parish in northeastern France for sixty years. Since the story of his life is so well known, it will not be repeated here.

The devotion of Kingsley and Oberlin to their parishes and their people, however, is one of the sublimest chapters in church history. They offered themselves a living sacrifice for their people, wholly and without reservation. They declined promotion as men regard promotion. They both declined parishes which offered them better pay. Their pay was better than gold. They were too absorbed in their work to be interested in worldly recognition or emoluments or denominational leadership of physical ease. They humbled themselves in doing a great task, and God honored them and blessed their labors and gave them names which will shine forever with celestial fire against a dark firmament of selfishness, self-seeking, human misery, and need. And men today, challenged by their noble examples, are beginning to realize that ministers of the gospel have a holy ministry to the total life of their constituencies.

The concluding part of this chapter, therefore, pays tribute to some of those in our day who are seeking thus to minister to all the needs—physical, mental, and spiritual—of their people.

EUGENE SMATHERS

Eugene Smathers became the first full-time resident pastor of the Big Lick Presbyterian Church, U. S. A., in 1934. He had accepted the pastorate of this church along with some other small churches upon completing his seminary work in 1932. The Big Lick community, which is located in the Cumberland Mountains of Tennessee, has a population of some fifty-odd families, or around three hundred souls. The average cash income per family in 1939 was only $230, and the average value of the rural dwellings was between $250 and $500.

Big Lick is fourteen miles from Crossville, the county seat and the only other town in the county. The nearest highway is two miles away, and the country roads are impassable much of the year. Not until recently has there been a telephone in the community, and there are only a few automobiles and radios.

For fifteen years prior to the coming of Smathers to Big Lick, Mrs. Carrie Murphy, a community worker, had served the community. A school building was used for such church services as were held.

The first major undertaking of this young pastor was the building of a house of worship. A leading layman of his denomination interested in Cumberland County agreed to furnish the money necessary for the material if the community would do the work. The labor was done by volunteer workers, with the pastor, who had never had any building experience, as the overseer. On May 30, 1935, a beautiful church on a hill overlooking the community was dedicated to the worship of God. This beautiful building, part stone and part frame, provides a worshipful sanctuary, adequate church-school facilities, a kitchen, a social room for recreational and other community activities, and a place for a community library.

Twenty-three acres of land were secured along with the church to be developed into a church farm and used for demonstration purposes. The church farm also helped to provide better support for the pastor. The size of this farm has since been increased to seventy acres.

The building of the Big Lick Church with volunteer labor gave the Big Lick community its first real lesson in co-operative effort for the benefit of the entire community and proved a most invaluable lesson.

A health center was needed. Because of the distance a physician had to travel, a doctor's visit cost from ten to fifteen dollars. Oftentimes a family had to sell their only cow or mortgage their small acreage to pay for one brief visit by a physician. Doctors were never called until the need seemed imperative, and then it was often too late. So the second major task of this pastor was a community health program for his people. The people being unable to pay for a nurse, the Mission Board provided for her salary. This added service called for a health center, and the friend who had made the church possible agreed again to furnish the money if the people would do the work. So the Warren H. Wilson House of Health was built in 1937. Here two clinics are held each month, a mother and baby clinic and a general medical clinic. Classes in first aid, home hygiene, and infant care are conducted regularly. And there are a few beds for emergency purposes.

A third achievement was the organization of a farmers' association. Farm machinery and better farm supplies were needed, but the people were not able to buy them. Eight farmers joined the farmers' association, which now has a membership of twenty-five. Together they have bought a grain drill, a tractor, plow, disc, power mower, lime spreader, corn planter, hammer mill for making feed, a sawmill, a cordwood saw, and a dragsaw. They have a working agreement by which all of the co-operating farmers may use the machinery. A machine operator has been employed, and work is done for many.

In 1940 this aggressive young pastor began a homesteading project. Some seventeen hundred acres of land were bought and resold in smaller plots at the price paid per acre for the large tract. As a result of this project young people have been able to establish themselves in homes of their own upon the land and have become an asset to both the community and the church.

In summary Smathers adds:

Since 1943 we have been an area project in soil conservation which makes possible more rapid community development through assistance in guidance and materials. And we have just started another demonstration project in co-operation with the Extension Service, that of a woodwork shop. . . . We expect rural electrification within the year, and this is going to mean much to our community and to our work.

Calvin Schnucker

Calvin Schnucker at the age of twenty-seven became pastor of the Ramsey Reformed Church on the open prairie near Titinka, Iowa, in 1935, the depth of the last great depression when three hundred churches in Iowa alone closed their doors and only 33 per cent of the farmers in the community owned their farms. The church, which had carried a mortgage since 1894, was a typical box-shaped, wooden structure that had not been painted for fifteen years. The window sills had rotted out, and it was very difficult to heat in winter. The parsonage was in little better condition.

The congregation was composed of elderly people who with few exceptions frowned on new ideas. Young people were conspicuous by their absence from services.

The young pastor sensed the need for a new and radical type of ministry to save the church and the community from disintegration. He became a full-fledged agricultural propagandist. His sermons glorified rural life. His personal interviews emphasized the desirability of the farm for personal satisfaction and for the rearing of children. His club talks and casual conversation sounded the same note of rural charm.

Homes were breaking up, and men were losing their farms. He made a careful study of land ownership, mortgages, and tenancy within a seven-mile radius of his church. He discovered that insurance companies held mortgages on many of the farms and personally went to see them. He got them to accept small down payments and installments which his farmer members could pay. He personally got other mortgage holders to cut their demands and ease their terms. He guided tenants in the buying of farms and by the fall of 1942 saw sixty families well established on owner-operated farms. About five hundred people were thus aided on their way to happy homes.

The church boomed. Young people swarmed in. All sorts of clubs were formed, including a young people's club with seventy members.

The young people went to work. They organized and ran a Sunday school twenty-three miles away. They built a lovely lawn about the church and turned a former chicken lot into an acre of grass and flowers. They leveled off and graveled another acre as a parking area. Twice a year they varnished and repaired the church furniture and fixed up the interior of the church. And there was not a case of juvenile delinquency in his parish during his pastorate!

He organized a co-operative to bring rural electrification to his people. He personally counseled his people on matrimonial matters and refused to marry elopers. When his people, young and old, needed medical advice or help, he secured it for them. He led his congregation in building a new church edifice which is valued at $35,000, but which actually cost only $17,000. And it is modern in every particular. Not afraid of work he put on his overalls and wired the church himself, saving his congregation $700. In nine years his church families increased from 72 to 144, his Sunday school from 70 to 375, his church attendance from 50 to 400.

What this young minister accomplished in one country church can be accomplished in many other country churches by wise, purposeful, determined, consecrated leadership, where the pastor refuses to leave before his job is done. Like others referred to he had tempting offers to better paying churches, but he refused to leave until he had completed his task.

Schnucker is now at the University of Dubuque training young ministers for the country church and giving advice to parishes on how to work out of their difficulties. He summarizes his aims as follows:

I don't want to waste time or effort on any city-bent young preacher who takes a rural pastorate simply as a steppingstone to a bigger parish call. A country church is big enough for any man who really wants to serve. And he can have a hand in developing the world's first industry and enjoy the company of the world's finest folk, the farmers.

C. Edwin Murphy

C. Edwin Murphy, pastor of the Crawford Valley and Stark Valley Churches in Nebraska, graduated from Drew Seminary in 1942. In December, 1945, he was called back to Drew for a reception given by some fifty theological students who were majoring in rural work and was designated by them as their "Pastor of the Year."

135

This is a student affair, and Murphy is the third student thus honored; but it is certainly a step in the right direction. Men who devote their lives to rural work on a sacrificial basis, most of them without the conveniences and comforts of their city brethren, are certainly deserving of special recognition. Other student and even denominational groups would do well to give special recognition in some form to someone each year who is rendering exceptionally intelligent and comprehensive service in the rural field.

Murphy has declined offers in New York City and in Lincoln, the capital of his home state, to serve the rural people of Nebraska. He is a good example of a large number of young men who are today dedicating themselves to the rural field. In his college and seminary days he took courses on the rural church, rural church finances, applied and rural sociology, rural social trends, and other kindred subjects. He set forth his views as follows:

I have the fullest intention of remaining with the rural church. The country is a good place to live. We do not have the competition with secularism in the country churches that we do in urban churches. I can function here as a leader and devote my time to the most important area of the church's work—young adults, youth, and children. We have our problems and discouragements, but most of these can be solved if a pastor is willing to stay long enough. I am not a rural preacher because I feel sorry for country folk. I do not feel that I am condescending or sacrificing to be a rural pastor. I am glad to be a country preacher. My wife and I are accepted as friends and neighbors in the community. We are Ed and Ann to the adults, youth, and children. We have broken down to a large degree the wall which so often separates a minister from his laymen.

With such a spirit Ed and Ann are sure to succeed. What has he done? A pastor cannot do a great deal in four years, but here is how he is working at his job. In addition to caring for the "spiritual life" of his people, preaching, holding Youth Fellowship meetings, directing choirs, visiting the sick, leading in recreational activities, hauling twelve to twenty children in his car over muddy roads to church, he is actively engaged in other programs for community betterment. He states:

I feel that my first responsibility is to my churches, but I am interested in other community agencies. I helped start a program of testing for Bang's disease in the community. The disease is now under control.

I am a member of the Dairy Breeders' Association. I was selected to serve in organizing the group because I could qualify as a dairyman. I have one cow! And the president pays my membership fees.

I serve on a soil conservation committee. It is a fascinating field, and I feel that the rural minister, if he is to preach stewardship, must know something about soil conservation.

He is now working on organizing a Four-H club, getting a public health nurse, and introducing music into the public schools of his community. In co-operation with other local pastors, he is advocating released-time religious instruction in the high school.

Ed Murphy is more than a preacher. He is a pastor and a community leader, and I predict for him an interesting and successful ministry.

137

Thomas C. Huff

Thomas C. Huff, a pastor of Jasper, Arkansas, has been presented the C. E. Palmer Award for Distinguished Citizenship for 1946 by the Arkansas State Junior Chamber of Commerce. What has young Huff done as a rural pastor to merit this recognition?

Jasper is the county seat of Newton County, which is located in the Heart-of-the-Ozarks section. It is "one of the most beautiful spots in the world," as the pastor describes it. But it is also one where natural isolation, poor roads, and poverty have cramped the opportunities of the people.

On June 1, 1943, young Huff, a graduate of Hendrix College, Conway, Arkansas, and Perkins School of Theology of Southern Methodist University, Dallas, Texas, was given all of Newton County with a "once-a-month" preaching appointment at Jasper.

The county has no railroad and only three miles of pavement across its most progressive corner. The church at Jasper was organized as a county-wide church in order that persons in isolated parts might be a part of the fellowship. Many people live in sections that cannot be reached by car. One country school, which has but a three-months' term, can be reached only by walking two miles. Huff has since completed a beautiful stone church at Jasper and established preaching appointments in eight other communities.

He conducts a youth camp each summer at Diamond Cave for Newton County young people. They bring their own groceries and share in the work, which enables him to keep the fee low enough for the young people from the poor mountain farms to attend.

In 1945 a little loyal group in the Basin community planted a Lord's Acre of tomatoes which cleared $110.

Two men have been licensed to preach: Carl F. Wood, an older man who will both farm and preach, holding services in "way back," hard-to-get-to communities; and Edgal Holt, a native of Newton County recently returned from service with the Marine Corps. Arrangements have been made for him to complete his high-school work at Jasper. He will then go to college to prepare himself to be a more effective minister, but meanwhile he is helping with the work in Newton County.

But Huff believes he is called to minister to the total life of his people. He initiated the organization of a chamber of commerce at Jasper, which proposes to clear the county of its sometimes undeserved reputation as "backwoodsy." The chamber of commerce is endeavoring to get a paved highway through the center of the county and to secure a lime crusher. Huff is secretary of the chamber of commerce.

Since the goat thrives on these rocky hillsides which wash away when crops are planted, this young pastor has interested himself in the development of a dairy goat industry. A number of new herds of better quality goats have been brought into the county. The pastor himself, in partnership with one of his superintendents, has purchased a small herd of registered goats, hoping to demonstrate what a herd of dairy goats can do. Their buck is available to help improve the herds of other farmers. A group of Italian cheese makers have been interested in putting a goat cheese factory in Jasper, which will provide a wonderful market for goat milk. More and more the people are coming to feel that the dairy goat industry can raise the standard of living for Newton County farmers and that there is no reason the county should not become the dairy goat capital of North America.

A great number of other college-trained young ministers who are proceeding along similar lines could be mentioned. These young ministers have caught their inspiration from Kingsley or Oberlin or the great need of modern rural life and with vision and no fear of work and with a program ministering to the total life of their constituencies are pointing the way to a new day in rural church life.

The rural pastor today has one of the biggest and most important jobs in the modern church, one which calls for initiative and unusual resourcefulness. No one rural minister could do all the things that have been suggested; perhaps all of them are not needed in every situation. Only such ideas and suggestions as may seem most feasible and necessary in the particular field should be adopted and adapted. These young men have proved that the suggestions offered in these chapters are practical and workable. What these have done, others can do. What these have done, others must do to rehabilitate and re-establish the church as a dynamic moral and religious force in American rural life.

Bibliography

BOOKS

Bailey, L. H. *The Holy Earth.* New York: Christian Rural Fellowship, 1943.

Beard, Augustus F. *The Story of John Frederic Oberlin.* Chicago: The Pilgrim Press, 1909.

Brunner, Edmund de S. *Working with Rural Youth.* Washington, D. C.: American Council on Education, 1942.

Butler, George D. *Introduction to Community Recreation.* New York: McGraw-Hill Book Co., Inc., 1940.

Cain, B. H. *The Church Ministering to Rural Life.* Dayton, Ohio: Otterbein Press, 1941.

Dawber, Mark A. *Rebuilding Rural America.* New York: Friendship Press, 1937.

Harbin, Elvin O. *Recreational Materials and Methods.* Nashville: Cokesbury Press, 1931.

Jacks, Graham V. and Whyte, L. O. *Vanishing Lands.* New York: Doubleday, Doran & Co., 1939.

Ligutti, Luigi G. and Rawe, John C. *Rural Roads to Security.* Milwaukee: Bruce Publishing Co., 1940.

Lindstrom, David E. *The Church in Rural Life.* Champaign, Ill.: Garrard Press, 1939.

Manifesto on Rural Life, National Catholic Rural Life Conference report. Milwaukee: Bruce Publishing Co., 1939.

May, Mark A. *The Education of American Ministers.* Institute of Social and Religious Research, 1934.

Mickey, Karl B. *Man and the Soil.* Chicago: International Harvester Co., 1945.

Moore, Arthur. *The Farmer and the Rest of Us.* Boston: Little, Brown and Co., 1945.

Morgan, Arthur E. *The Small Community.* New York: Harper and Brothers, 1942.

Powell, W. T. *Recreation in Church and Community.* New York: Abingdon Press, 1938.

Richardson, Norman E. *The Church at Play*. New York: Abingdon Press, 1922.

Rochester, Anna. *Why Farmers Are Poor*. New York: International Publishers, 1940.

Sanderson, Ezra D. and Polson, Robert A. *Rural Community Organization*. New York: John Wiley and Sons, Inc., 1939.

Sanderson, Ezra D. *Leadership for Rural Life*. New York: Association Press, 1940.

Schmidt, Carl T. *American Farmers in the World Crisis*. New York: Oxford University Press, 1941.

Smith, Rockwell C. *The Church in Our Town*. New York and Nashville: Abingdon-Cokesbury Press, 1945.

Sundt, Edwin E. *The Country Church and Our Generation*. New York: Flemming H. Revell Co., 1932.

Tipple, Ezra. *Some Famous Country Parishes*. New York: Abingdon Press, 1911.

Waring, P. Alston and Teller, Walter M. *Roots in the Earth*. New York: Harper and Brothers, 1943.

Wrenn, C. Gilbert and Harley, D. L. *Time on Their Hands*. Washington, D. C.: American Council on Education, 1941.

PAMPHLETS

American Council on Education. *Guide Posts for Rural Youth*.

Arvold, Alfred G., Extension Service, North Dakota Agricultural College, Fargo, N. D. *Neighborhood Activities in Country Communities*.

Dana, Malcolm. *The Larger Parish*.

Department of Town and Country Church, The Methodist Church. *The Changing Small Church*.

———. *The Group Ministry Plan*.

———. *The Methodist Church in Town and Country*.

Felton, Ralph A. *The Church Farm*.

———. *The Lord's Acre*.

———. *The Salary of Rural Pastors*.

Future Farmers of America, Revised Manual. Baltimore, Md.: French-Bray Printing Co.

Home Missions Council of America. *Urgent Tasks for the Town and Country Church*.

BIBLIOGRAPHY

————. *What Emphasis for Town and Country Church.*
McClure, James G. K. *Lord's Acre Plan Succeeds.*
Rich, Mark. *The Larger Parish.*

U. S. DEPT. OF AGRICULTURE BULLETINS

Achieving a Balanced Agriculture.
Agricultural Finance Review. November, 1946.
Arbor Day, Its Purpose and Observance. Bulletin 1492.
Care of Ornamental Trees and Shrubs. Bulletin 1826.
Disadvantaged Classes in American Agriculture.
Farm Income Situation.
Getting at the Facts About Agriculture.
Getting Established on the Land.
Wages of Agricultural Labor in the United States.

PUBLIC HEALTH BULLETINS

Social Security Board. *Need for Medical Care Insurance.* April, 1944.
————. *Prepayment Medical Care Organizations.* Memorandum No. 55.
U. S. Dept. of Agriculture. *Better Health for Rural America.* 1945.
————. *Hospitals for Rural Communities.* Bulletin 1792.
U. S. Dept. of Labor. *Births, Infant Mortality, Maternal Mortality.*
————. *Childhood Mortality from Accidents.* Publication No. 311.
————. *Maternal and Child Health Service.* Publication No. 259.
————. *Services for Crippled Children.* Publication No. 258.
————. *Standards of Child Health, Education, and Social Welfare.* Publication No. 287.
U. S. Public Health Service. *Rural Sewage Disposal.*
————. *Rural Water Supply Sanitation.*

SPECIAL RURAL PUBLICATIONS

The Christian Rural Fellowship Bulletin
Methodist Rural Fellowship Bulletin
Town and Country Church Bulletin

143